THE DIVINE COUNSELOR

THE DIVINE COUNSELOR

RENEW YOUR MIND, HEAL YOUR SOUL, AND DISCOVER YOUR PURPOSE THROUGH THE GUIDANCE OF THE HOLY SPIRIT

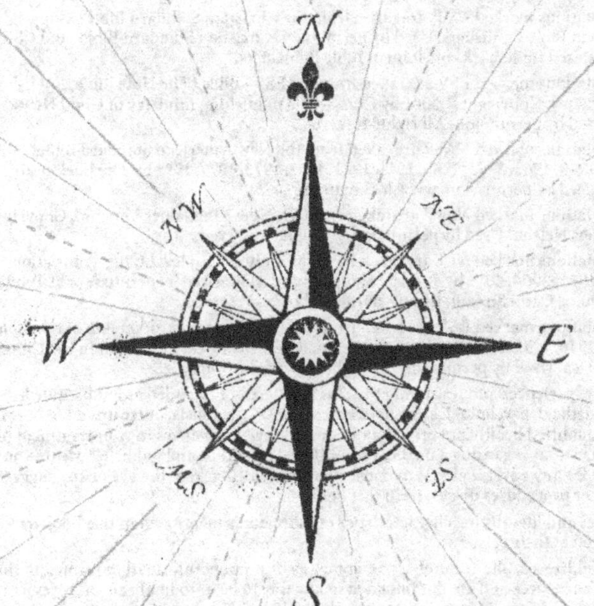

ALEX SEELEY

An Imprint of Thomas Nelson

The Divine Counselor

Published by Nelson Books, an imprint of Thomas Nelson, 501 Nelson Place, Nashville, TN 37214, USA. Nelson Books and Thomas Nelson are registered trademarks of HarperCollins Christian Publishing, Inc.

The author is represented by Alive Literary Agency, www.aliveliterary.com.

Thomas Nelson titles may be purchased in bulk for educational, business, fundraising, or sales promotional use. For information, please email SpecialMarkets@ThomasNelson.com.

The personal experiences and testimonies in this book are not intended as a substitute for professional medical, psychological, or psychiatric advice, diagnosis, or treatment. Always consult your qualified healthcare provider before making any changes to your treatment plan or with any questions regarding a medical condition. The author and publisher assume no responsibility for any adverse effects or consequences resulting from the use of any suggestions, preparations, or procedures discussed in this book.

Certain names and identifying characteristics of individuals mentioned in this book have been changed to protect their privacy.

Any internet addresses, phone numbers, or company or product information printed in this book are offered as a resource and are not intended in any way to be or to imply an endorsement by Thomas Nelson, nor does Thomas Nelson vouch for the existence, content, or services of these sites, phone numbers, companies, or products beyond the life of this book.

ISBN 978-1-4002-5528-3 (audiobook)
ISBN 978-1-4002-5526-9 (ePub)
ISBN 978-1-4002-5496-5 (TP)

HarperCollins Publishers, Macken House, 39/40 Mayor Street Upper, Dublin 1, D01 C9W8, Ireland (https://www.harpercollins.com)

Library of Congress Control Number: 2026934232

978-1-4002-5496-5

Art direction: Curt Diepenhorst
Cover design by Avenir Creative House
Cover illustration: Roberto Scandola / iStock
Interior Design: Kristy Edwards

Printed in the United States of America
26 27 28 29 30 LBC 7 6 5 4 3

To Holy Spirit, I pray that these words reveal just how divine You truly are. Thank You for being my very best friend.

CONTENTS

INTRODUCTION

Have you ever imagined being alive when Jesus was on the earth? To see blind eyes open, deaf ears hear, dead bodies come back to life, and demons cower in submission to the power of Jesus Christ? To witness firsthand how He navigated persecution and betrayal? To sit at His feet and receive all of His revelation as He unpacked the Scriptures? To listen to conversations where He confounded the religious spirit? To watch Him pray and connect with the Father and learn how He overcame grief and disappointment when those He loved died and those He trusted betrayed Him? To see Him face-to-face and have access to His wisdom and instruction 24/7—the omniscient God who knows every detail of humanity and has the perfect answer for every issue we face? The disciples walked closely with Him, and yet they were scarcely aware that God Himself was in their midst—the promise of Emmanuel, "God with us," made flesh and dwelling among them.

Jesus, fully man and fully God, lived in complete submission to both the Father and the Holy Spirit. He modeled what it means to be led by the Spirit of God. He taught us how to walk as sons and daughters within His kingdom, with renewed minds that overcome life's challenges and live abundantly and with great purpose. I often find myself asking the question, "What would Jesus do in this situation right now?" Can you imagine having Him next to you, in the flesh, as you face life's most difficult problems?

The Bible tells us that He was tempted in every way and yet did not sin. He overcame every trial and test with wisdom and power. He did nothing apart from the Father and, by the power of the Holy Spirit, He lived a perfect life here on earth. He spent three and a half years teaching and training His disciples to live with a new kingdom mindset, all while knowing that He would leave them with the assignment to go into all the world, make disciples, and build His church.

Jesus knew His disciples could not live life in abundance and fulfill their assignment on earth without Him, and neither can we. So He promised to never leave them without His power or presence. He said it was better for Him to go so that the *Counselor* could come into close fellowship with them. John 14:16 says, "And I will ask the Father, and He will give you another Helper (Comforter, Advocate, Intercessor—Counselor, Strengthener, Standby), to be with you forever" (AMP).

Jesus was limited in His body to time, space, and geography while here on earth, and even though He knew He had to go back to the Father and would no longer be able to walk with the disciples in the flesh, He promised another Helper, another Counselor. He said, "I will not leave you as orphans; I will come to you" (John 14:18). He vowed that the Holy Spirit would now be the same Counselor and Helper—just not in fleshly form.

The Greek word for Counselor is *paraklétos* (*paraclete*), which means one who is called alongside.[1] Jesus kept His word by ensuring that we would always have a person of the triune God to guide, teach, comfort, and walk alongside us—reminding us of all Jesus spoke and helping us to correctly discern His will. The Holy Spirit is the Spirit of Christ, God on earth.

After His resurrection and before His ascension to heaven,

Jesus said, "I am going to send you what my Father has promised; but stay in the city until you have been clothed with power from on high" (Luke 24:49).

Why would He instruct His disciples *not to leave* Jerusalem until they had the Holy Spirit? You may have heard this called "the baptism of the Holy Spirit" or "being filled with the Spirit." Jesus was about to baptize them in the Holy Spirit, which would give them supernatural power to live as Christians, just like when the Holy Spirit descended on Jesus at His water baptism before He began His ministry on earth. He knew they would need the same power and authority to be effective witnesses for the kingdom and to endure the trials that were certain to come. And so do we.

He anticipated the days when the disciples would ask, "What would Jesus do if He were here with us?" He refused to leave them without answers, just as He won't leave us to stumble in the dark. He sent the Holy Spirit to be our Counselor and friend—the One who never leaves our side and is always ready to answer us when we cry out to Him.

Sadly, many Christians either do not understand what it means to be filled and empowered by the Holy Spirit or they underestimate the necessity of needing the Holy Spirit actively working in their lives so they can live righteously and victoriously. The infilling of the Holy Spirit is not a one-time experience. We need the awareness of His presence in our lives on a daily basis. Our world is filled with Christians who struggle through life, even in the best of times. Many are tormented with confusion, anxiety, depression, and fear, which only serve to keep them stuck in a rut of mental and emotional strongholds. These cycles keep us from the life of freedom that is available to us through the resurrection power of Jesus, which is the power of the Holy Spirit. When our lives are controlled by our emotions or the untreated effects of past trauma, we quickly forget that we have *full* access to God Himself and all His wisdom—just as the disciples did—with all His power and authority.

Feelings and emotions are great servants, but they are terrible masters. While they can be important tools and often alert us to something deeper, they can also be unreliable guides that lead us into dark places of despair, destruction, and depression. This is why it is crucial to become Spirit-led as Christ followers. We have a spirit man inside us who, when submitted to the lordship of Christ, will help us overcome all temptations, struggles, and controlling mindsets. We must know the truth and the truth will set us free.

So, how do we get to know the truth? How do we live a life of freedom, fulfillment, and purpose? We get to know Jesus Christ through the power of the Holy Spirit. The Holy Spirit reveals the truth through God's Word and helps us develop an intimate relationship with Jesus. If we have been given a Divine Counselor in the Holy Spirit, why wouldn't we depend on His wisdom and instruction to help us in our lives? Let's be honest: We need all the help we can get.

After more than thirty years of pastoring, I can say that many Christians have not tapped into the most powerful source available to us. This is why so many individuals are not living up to their full potential and struggle to live in complete freedom. Too many are attempting to navigate life in their own strength, relying on the flesh rather than being empowered by the Holy Spirit. That is not how God intended for us to live. Galatians 5:1 reminds us, "It is for freedom that Christ has set us free."

The Holy Spirit was sent by God to be in close fellowship with us, walking and talking with us as if God were with us in the flesh. This brings us back to the garden where life began in perfect harmony between God and mankind. In Eden, God walked with Adam, building a relationship with him, guiding him, and instructing him. However, the Enemy deceived Adam and Eve into believing they could gain wisdom and knowledge to become "like God" by eating from the Tree of Knowledge of Good and Evil (Genesis 3:5). Giving in to this temptation only brought chaos and confusion to their identities and relationship with God. This act introduced brokenness and independence from God into the world. Now, because of sin, we must live with the consequences of being separated from the perfect counsel of God.

Despite the hopelessness sin brought, God Almighty had a plan to restore hope. His plan was Jesus Christ—His one and only Son—who would come to earth, die on the cross, and rise again to reconcile us back to the original design of intimate relationship with the Father. He never intended for us to be separated from Him. God's intention has always been for us to live free of shame, guilt, trauma, and sin. The Holy Spirit has been given to us as our Divine Counselor, Helper, Teacher, Guide, and Comforter. But when we fail to seek Him for the answers we desperately need, it shouldn't come as a surprise why we struggle to overcome life's challenges. I don't believe it is for lack of desire. Rather, it may be because we've never been taught how to connect with the person of the Holy Spirit. We need to get to know Him, learn how to hear His voice, follow His instruction, and obey Him when He asks us to do the work required to build resilience.

The Holy Spirit has every solution to all our problems. He

is the Divine Counselor who carries supernatural power and enables us to overcome. We have direct access to Him through Jesus, enabling us to live victoriously in this world. This only happens, however, when we know Him—not just read about Him as if He were a thing rather than a person.

The Holy Spirit is God in Spirit, the Spirit of Christ is the Holy Spirit, and the Holy Spirit is the Spirit of Christ (Romans 8:9–10). The Holy Spirit is here, desiring to live and dwell within us, leading and guiding us into all truth, and setting us up for victory in every area of our lives. He not only wants to walk with us through every crisis we face, but He also wants to be our perfect counselor, instructing and empowering us to live our daily lives. The Holy Spirit guides us through the sanctification process after salvation. *Sanctification* simply means "the process of being set apart, made holy, and made suitable for God's use, encompassing both a past act of being declared righteous and a present, ongoing process of becoming more like Christ through the power of the Holy Spirit."[2]

The Holy Spirit helps us become more like Jesus through His conviction, guidance, and instruction, which we will talk more about in the following chapters. Most important, He desires to be our best friend, not just our teacher. Proverbs 18:24 says, "But there is a friend who sticks closer than a brother," referring to both Jesus and the Holy Spirit.

As these pages unfold, you will read real-life stories from me and from those I have personally walked with—stories of people who allowed the Divine Counselor to transform them in supernatural ways. The same Spirit of God who led them into freedom can lead you in all truth—24/7, every day of the year—answering questions you thought had no answers and healing the deep wounds you are trying to heal. He is the Divine Counselor, He is peace, and He is truth. He is what we are all looking for but have been searching for in all the wrong places.

I am living proof that you can access the Divine Counselor and be changed from the inside out. My life has been transformed. I experienced generational patterns of abuse and rejection that led to addiction, oppression, and self-loathing. Yet with the help of the Divine Counselor, the Holy Spirit, and through time spent listening to and obeying His voice, I am a living testimony that you can live life free of pain and truly live a life abundantly in Christ Jesus, as Scripture promises. We know that "the thief comes only to steal and kill and destroy" but I'm so thankful for the latter part of that verse because Jesus said, "I have come that they may have life, and have it to the full" (John 10:10).

This doesn't mean that life is free of troubles when you become a Christian. If that is what you have been told, you will be sadly disappointed. The Bible says, "In this world you *will* have trouble" (emphasis mine). However, when trouble comes in my life, instead of falling into a pit of despair and destruction, I choose to remember that the end of the verse says, "But take heart! I have overcome the world" (John 16:33).

It's now up to me to seek and apply the counsel I have received. Because He has already overcome, I can walk with Him, through surrendered obedience to His Word, through each difficulty, and to overcome too. I have become resilient and strong through the struggles of my life instead of being overcome by the heaviness that life can bring. I am living a life I never imagined could be this blessed. I can confidently say, I am an overcomer!

Like all of us, I have access to supernatural peace and spiritual authority in Christ. I have learned how to cast my cares on

Him because He cares for me. I have learned by the power of the Holy Spirit how to calm anxious thoughts. He has delivered me from addiction, self-loathing, and a spirit of fear. He has given me a sound mind and led me to freedom in every area of my life.

Now I live my life preaching and teaching about the love of Jesus and the power of the Holy Spirit to bring deliverance to those who are bound. I have seen the kindness of God deliver thousands of people and I will spend the rest of my life preaching the truth of God's Word that sets people free. I invite you into this journey of discovering the Holy Spirit as your Divine Counselor. Through revelation of the Scriptures and practical application, you can experience the freedom you have so desperately been searching for.

You are not alone, and you were never meant to scramble through life trying to make it work on your own. Scripture says, "Trust in the Lord with all your heart and lean not on your own understanding; in all your ways submit to him, and he will make your paths straight" (Proverbs 3:5–6). As you surrender your whole heart and choose to lean on His wisdom and understanding instead of the world's system, He will turn the chaos in your life into peace and give you a beautiful life.

CHAPTER 1

The Pendulum Swing

When we first started meeting in the basement of our home in 2012 before The Belonging Co had a name and it was just a small Bible study, I discovered that many of the men and women attending came from faith backgrounds very different from how I grew up. I quickly realized they also struggled to relate to God in a personal and intimate way. They went to church and most of them did some form of daily Bible reading, but many of them were bound with strongholds they could not break free from. My heart moved with compassion as I looked at so many church attendees who were harassed by their anxious thoughts and felt helpless to overcome their addictions. I knew that my husband, Henry, and I were there for a purpose: to help them discover the freedom found in Jesus through the power of the Holy Spirit.

I took for granted that everyone had been taught about the Holy Spirit and why He is imperative if we want to live as victorious followers of Christ. But there were many people on opposite ends of the spectrum when it came to understanding the Holy Spirit. Some were familiar with His person and work while others were completely unaware of His presence and power. I suddenly felt the weight of the responsibility of teaching them not only who the person of the Holy Spirit is, but also the power He has to transform them from the inside out—something most had never learned in the churches they attended.

Some had been taught that the Holy Spirit was bad and not to be engaged with. Others had been told that the gifts of the Spirit ceased after the time of the apostles. Some were told that speaking in tongues was not of God. Others were afraid of this mystical force that seemed more ghostlike than deity, and His reputation was likened to the crazy uncle you try to avoid at family functions. But honestly, they had never sat in a service where they experienced a personal encounter with the Holy Spirit—until they saw God tangibly move in our basement. They could not articulate what was happening to them at the time, but the result of those encounters brought freedom and deliverance to their lives in a supernatural way. It was a new revelation that forever marked and changed them.

Not only did they notice the change, but everyone in their sphere noticed it too. That is why our home was packed every Tuesday night—because of this phenomenon of the power of the Holy Spirit moving in people's lives. Over the years, we have had so many people ask, "Why was this never taught to us growing up?" Many others have told us, "I wish I had been introduced to the Holy Spirit sooner. I would have had a different experience with God and my faith would have looked very different. Maybe I wouldn't have made so many mistakes because of following rules and regulations without revelation if I had known about His presence and power."

Testimonies were pouring in from people who truly encountered God's presence through the power of His Spirit. They shared stories of addictions being broken, deep disappointments being healed at the root, and marriages being restored. Some who had suffered abuse as children experienced healing over time that enabled them to forgive their abusers. Those riddled with irrational fear were set free and those serving in full-time ministry felt like they were coming alive in their faith. It was as if they were being resuscitated.

It was like the breath of God—the *ruach* (in Hebrew it means "breath," "spirit," or "wind")—was breathing His fresh breath of life back into their lungs, giving them a second wind.[1] They came alive with fresh purpose and destiny. This was the result of the Holy Spirit encountering each person in a very personal and gentle way. He spoke to each heart, revealing supernatural wisdom and truth that brought deliverance and freedom on an individual level.

One evening I felt led to teach about being baptized in the Holy Spirit, described in the book of Acts, which I will explain in detail for you in chapter 6. I began to share with them that Jesus promised us the Holy Spirit and that He is more than just a wind, a force, or a ghost as some had heard. Rather, He is the Spirit of God, given to empower us to live with power and authority as believers. As I concluded, I asked if anyone wanted to be baptized in the Holy Spirit and receive their heavenly prayer language. Many came forward and were immediately filled with the Spirit as we prayed for them while others encountered God in a new and powerful way. However, there was a couple—a young man and young woman—who looked like deer caught in headlights. They just stood there staring, paralyzed by fear. I quickly discerned that something deeper was going on, so I walked over and quietly asked if they were okay.

The gentleman responded, "Not really. You see, we had a terrible experience in college when we asked for prayer to be baptized in the Holy Spirit. It was one of the most humiliating and traumatic experiences we have ever had. People were shouting and screaming over us saying, 'Be filled!' It felt like we were being forced to have an experience we didn't understand. We left that night feeling overwhelmed and ashamed because nothing happened. They made it seem to everyone else in the room like we had been filled, but we hadn't. We never went back and have been avoiding anything slightly 'charismatic' since then."

I remember feeling such sadness when I heard their story. It broke my heart. First, because that is not how God operates; and second, because as I continued on this journey of discipleship with those who were attending our Tuesday night meetings, I began to realize they weren't the only ones. I've heard countless traumatic experiences about people being prayed for, especially in charismatic churches. I believe this is why so many have completely swung to the opposite extreme. They were so traumatized by their negative encounters that instead of seeking authentic truth, they reject the concept altogether. In doing so, they miss a facet of God essential for our Christian walk.

When a person or an entire generation is negatively impacted by an experience, there's often a tendency to overcorrect. We end up swinging the pendulum too far in the opposite direction. We not only remove what needs adjusting but set aside what is good. In our overreaction, we end up throwing out the good along with the bad. When a culture or movement swings to extremes, it is often a protective mechanism that says, "I can't allow this to happen to me ever again, so I will do the exact opposite in order to safeguard my heart and shield myself from pain." The problem is that pendulum swings are always reactionary. If we keep living in reaction, it becomes harder to discern the truth from the lie.

Many believers are torn between two extremes. On one hand, there are those who experienced a performance that brought only confusion and harm to their relationship with God. Many who grew up witnessing over-the-top, exaggerated displays, such as being pushed over to make it seem like the power of God was present, along with strange manifestations, were left with deep church wounds. These experiences caused them to feel as though they were being pressured into believing something that wasn't real. As a result, you have the other extreme. There are those who have ignored the movement of the Holy Spirit altogether due to fear or lack of understanding. They made personal vows to avoid anything related to the Holy Spirit.

I think this is what's happened in the church over time. During my thirteen years in the United States, the majority of Christians I have pastored did not have an active relationship with the Holy Spirit while growing up. They were taught about God and Jesus and were encouraged to memorize Scripture, but many of those verses simply remained words on a page that never brought much transformative power to their lives. The Holy Spirit was rarely mentioned in the churches they attended. They would read about the Holy Spirit in the New Testament, but they were never told that He is essential for their daily walk with God. To them, the Holy Spirit was just a force, a wind, a dove, or a symbol of God. How on earth could they relate or engage with that?

This is not a new reaction. It has happened throughout church history. In Acts 2, we read that the Holy Spirit was poured out at Pentecost around AD 30, and the outpouring of the Holy

Spirit was evident in the movement of the early church. Fast-forward to Acts 19, around AD 54, and we see things had already begun to swing in the opposite direction.

> While Apollos was at Corinth, Paul took the road through the interior and arrived at Ephesus. There he found some disciples and asked them, "Did you receive the Holy Spirit when you believed?"
>
> They answered, "No, we have not even heard that there is a Holy Spirit."
>
> So Paul asked, "Then what baptism did you receive?"
>
> "John's baptism," they replied.
>
> Paul said, "John's baptism was a baptism of repentance. He told the people to believe in the one coming after him, that is, in Jesus." On hearing this, they were baptized in the name of the Lord Jesus. When Paul placed his hands on them, the Holy Spirit came on them, and they spoke in tongues and prophesied. There were about twelve men in all. Paul entered the synagogue and spoke boldly there for three months, arguing persuasively about the kingdom of God. (Acts 19:1–8)

Only twenty-four years had passed, and the church in Ephesus did not even know about the Holy Spirit! Paul needed to reintroduce the church in Ephesus to being baptized in the Holy Spirit. Now, two thousand years later, many Christians are still asking who the Holy Spirit is and whether it is necessary to be baptized in the Holy Spirit. According to Scripture, the religious people condemned Jesus and the apostles for moving in the realm of the power of the Holy Spirit (or operating in the power of the Holy Spirit) through signs, wonders, and miracles.

Today, the religious spirit still hates the Holy Spirit moving actively within the church. It loves to control people's behavior through rules and rituals, and it often stands in the way of God moving freely in a person's life. Sadly, this feels similar to our current reality where some in the church are afraid of the Holy Spirit moving during our Sunday services, concerned it might frighten people away. As a result, church gatherings have become so seeker-friendly that we have forgotten the Spirit's power that is meant to be demonstrated and experienced.

The subject of the Holy Spirit has been a source of contention within the global church, causing breakdowns and divisions. These doctrinal differences have resulted in multiple denominations and stark arguments across the Christian church, creating great confusion for the world. A divided church cannot effectively reach a broken world. This division is another tool in the Enemy's toolbox—one we have willingly handed to him—intended to cause disunity and dissension. While we are busy arguing over our differences, the world is missing out on a united and powerful move of the Spirit of God that can radically transform lives and usher in His kingdom on earth, just as it did in the early church.

Imagine a church that walks and talks like Jesus did on earth. Imagine a church that moves in the same power of the early church, seeing miracles, signs, and wonders. A church that endures through hard times and brings glory to God instead of being overwhelmed by circumstances. A church that stands in unity about the very thing God has promised us. When I say "church," I don't mean the institution of religion but each one of us who makes up the church.

The biblical concept of church (Greek: *ekklésia*) refers to an assembly or gathering of people, not a physical building.[2] Now, imagine what we could accomplish as individuals within this body of believers if we truly understood that the Holy Spirit is not some mystical force that makes people weird. Instead, the Holy Spirit is the power that enables the church to function as beautifully as it was designed, with the supernatural power to bring heaven to earth as Jesus did.

This *is* possible because there is precedent in the Word of God. It's recorded in the Gospels and the book of Acts, and it is still happening across the earth within many individuals and churches. I truly believe no one desires boring religion; we all want to experience the fullness of God. Could it be that the Enemy has strategically introduced counterfeit experiences into some of our lives to make us reject the concept of the Holy Spirit entirely? And in doing so, he keeps us spiritually stunted and bound even though we've already been saved?

The issue is not a lack of desire. It's that so many have received misinformation that has caused our generation to miss out on what we actually need. The Bible is clear: The Holy Spirit is given to us to reveal truth and be our helper, but if we are not taught how to engage with the third person of the Godhead, we will continue to walk with God at a level that God never intended for us to live.

In today's church climate, we see a divided belief system—exacerbated by a lack of understanding and knowledge of the Holy Spirit as a person who carries the power to transform lives. Unfortunately, the way the Holy Spirit has been taught or presented to some has caused fear, rather than revealing the beauty of the gift we all have access to. As a result, many Christians with deep emotional wounds are coping instead of truly thriving.

When we develop coping mechanisms to treat symptoms rather than address root causes with the help of proper counsel and the power of the Holy Spirit, we miss the opportunity to become completely whole and healed.

We must acknowledge that we are fully human, and in accepting Jesus, we also become fully eternal. Both aspects of our identity must be embraced. To neglect either is to deny the fullness of who God created us to be. The Holy Spirit, when we invite Him, reveals the root of our pain. Yet, our humanity often requires a process—a journey of taking responsibility and healing. Sanctification often takes time in the presence of God, community, and godly counsel. While God can bring instant, supernatural healing, it is often through the ongoing process of understanding, following that initial encounter with Him, that the true work begins.

In this sacred journey, the Divine Counselor walks beside us. For some, healing will include the guidance of a trained counselor; for others, it may come through the love and support of friends, family, or community. When we take this personal responsibility, God is the ultimate Healer, but He invites us to participate in the healing too.

If every time a problem comes up and your first thought is, *I need to speak to my therapist*, that is not growth. It is dependency on a person to help you with the issues in your life. I do not believe it has to be an either-or when it comes to the ministry of the Holy Spirit and counseling. I believe it can be a both-and with the understanding that our full dependence must be on the Healer to bring lasting transformation to our lives. We must make sure that the emphasis is on allowing the Holy Spirit and the power of Jesus—the omniscient God—to bring freedom and deliverance from spiritual strongholds. These are strongholds that only Jesus can heal through the resurrection power of the cross.

Jesus came to earth to heal the brokenhearted, to set the captive free, and to release the oppressed. He did not come to earth to live for thirty-three years, defeat death, hell, and the grave for us to simply cope with life. He came so we could overcome, just as He overcame the world for us! As the apostle Paul stated, it was not by eloquent words that the early church was transformed, but by the power of the Holy Spirit.

> And my message and my preaching were not in persuasive words of wisdom [using clever rhetoric], but [they were delivered] in demonstration of the [Holy] Spirit [operating through me] and of [His] power [stirring the minds of the listeners and persuading them]. (1 Corinthians 2:4 AMP)

The apostle Paul was constantly leading the church into the truth of the gospel, ensuring they didn't stray or swing the pendulum through false doctrine or the influence of false prophets who added or subtracted from the gospel message. He encouraged the church to use wisdom and to always return to the truth. We must also be careful to do the same because we are all prone to swing to extremes when something is neglected or not cultivated properly.

WHEN I WANTED TO MOVE TO AN EXTREME DUE TO MY NEGATIVE EXPERIENCE

When I was a young girl, unmarried and without children, I remember making a vow that I would *never* discipline my children through spanking. The discipline I experienced growing up was extremely damaging and abusive. It had a massive negative effect on my self-esteem, and I didn't want to inflict that kind of trauma onto my children. However, as I received healing through the work of the Holy Spirit in my areas of trauma, I began to ask Him what godly parenting looked like. I asked the Holy Spirit to teach me, lead me, and guide me as I raised my children.

I also had to ask myself an important question: What is the biblical way to raise a family? I didn't want to react to my painful past experiences or repeat history subconsciously. Whatever does not get addressed or healed in our lives, we tend to repeat. I also sought out people around me who had raised well-behaved and emotionally healthy children and asked for their counsel. I didn't want to rely solely on my own ideas but instead sought wisdom from those who had good fruit in their own lives.

Rather than swing the pendulum in self-protection, I chose to ask the Lord what He thought. He led me through the Scriptures, instructing me on how to be led by the Holy Spirit in my parenting. The Holy Spirit is the greatest parent and knows far better than we ever will because He is God. Ultimately, He created my children and entrusted them to my husband and me to raise and steward well. If we learn to take time to read God's Word, be still in His presence, and listen to His voice, He will guide us into all truth and give us the wisdom that leads to peace. This allows us to live from a place of clarity and grace rather than living controlled by our emotions or dysfunction.

Have you ever said to yourself, "I will never be like so-and-so," yet found yourself becoming even worse than they were? Even though we may not intend to repeat what was done to us, if we don't uproot brokenness or deep pain, we will remain bound to our past. We will see through a broken lens, making decisions to appease our own conscience rather than living from a place of wholeness and a healed heart. This is why we need the Divine Counselor living within us—to help us navigate situations like these and so much more.

No matter how shallow or deep our issues may be, the Holy Spirit really does have the answer for every care and concern. He is willing and ready to give us wisdom and understanding. We simply need to be willing to release our own erratic and reactionary emotions and allow Him to lead according to His truth. He desires to deliver you from all fear and anxiety and replace it with a sound mind that functions at full capacity. This is what the Holy Spirit is designed to do in our everyday lives.

GENERATIONAL FREEDOM BEGINS WITH SAYING YES TO GOD

My mother became a Christian in the charismatic revival that took place in the 1970s. She was baptized in the Catholic Church as an infant, and although her family would say they were Catholic, they didn't really practice their faith in daily life. As a young girl, she would go to church sometimes with her uncle, and after Mass she would walk around the perimeter of the chapel, looking at the Stations of the Cross. She was deeply moved by the death of Jesus and would often ask God the big questions she had about her life. Yet even though she was moved by His sacrifice for her, she didn't feel like she could hear His voice, and she never would have thought to ask God a question and expect that He would answer. That was the role of the priest. He was the mediator and voice of God for the people. God felt distant and uninterested in what concerned her little heart. Her heart had been so bruised by disappointments and cruel words spoken over her. Still, she dreamed of a life that seemed better than the reality she knew as a young girl.

After immigrating to Australia when she was nineteen years old, she fell into a deep sadness. Away from home, she felt aimless and was afraid of being in a foreign country, separated from her parents. She married young and had children immediately after. By the time she had her third child, she was searching for more. Her life felt empty, overwhelming, and unfulfilled. At twenty-five, she became a born-again Christian and truly felt a change in her heart. She realized that Jesus had been walking with her ever since she was a little girl, and she made a commitment to follow Him all the days of her life.

Even though she had a radical encounter with Jesus and experienced a newness in her faith, she still struggled with her mental health. Her life had been filled with disappointment, abuse, anger, and rejection. Negative words spoken over her had deeply damaged her self-esteem. The skeletons of her past were locked up tight in the closet of her heart. She never spoke about her struggles or pain. Even though she had become a Christian and regularly attended church, she didn't feel safe to talk openly about what she was going through. To know my mum on the exterior was to know the life of the party. Her laughter was loud and contagious, and her hospitality knew no match. She would make everyone feel welcomed and loved cooking for days to prepare a feast for those she loved dearly. But behind that extroverted exterior was the deep pain that she was carrying alone in the depths of her broken heart.

During this era, admitting to emotional or mental health issues was considered extremely shameful. She often told herself, *Maybe these issues just have a way of working themselves out.* Please hear me, friend. The issues in our interior life never just "work themselves out." This is why I am so passionate about writing this book—because like myself for such a long time, I keep seeing men and women focus on building their exterior lives while neglecting their interior lives, which are crumbling and affecting not only them but the people around them. The issues of our past and the trauma we've experienced *must* be dealt with.

The issues in our interior life never just "work themselves out."

Because she didn't have the right counsel or proper tools, my mother experienced two nervous breakdowns by the time she was forty. She went to her family doctor, who prescribed sedatives to help "calm her nerves." The doctor mentioned that she should not drive while taking them, and my mother thought, *These must be powerful drugs.* When she returned home, she took one pill and later described the experience as feeling like she was moonwalking. Everything slowed down, and she felt completely unlike herself. When the effects of the drug wore off, she felt in her heart that the way forward was not simply numbing the pain she was in. She didn't like how it made her feel, and she realized she needed something stronger than medication to truly heal her. She felt the Holy Spirit say to her heart, *I want us to face the painful things of your past and walk together to the other side into freedom. If you'll let Me, I will lead you and I will heal the bruised, bloody, and broken places of your heart.*

In that moment, she made a decision that would forever change the trajectory of her life. She threw those pills in the trash and made a declaration to the Lord: "God, if You are telling me the truth, and if You heal my broken heart, I will do whatever it takes to walk in freedom." At that very moment, she asked God to show her the root of what was troubling her heart and through His Spirit, He brought revelation to her. He showed her the root of her disappointment: She had been robbed of her education at the age of ten. Her parents had pulled her out of school, and at that moment, a vital piece of her heart was ripped away.

As a young girl, she loved school dearly. It was her place of wonder, hope, and possibility. Being forced to leave the place she loved devastated her. From that point on, disappointments kept hitting her like a relentless tsunami, wave after wave crashing down with every decision that was made *for* her, not *by* her. Each blow stripped away more of her voice, her confidence, and her dreams, until she had no hope left in her heart. That grief didn't stay in childhood. It followed her into her young adult life, casting a shadow over every opportunity. Nothing ever seemed to fall in her favor. She felt trapped in a life she hadn't chosen, isolated and aching, as if the walls of her own heart had become a prison. There was no one to talk to in the small town she was from.

During the time she was attending church, there was a common belief that if you were a Christian, then God had dealt with everything in your life at salvation, and from that point on, you were completely fine. You would greet your fellow congregant members with salutations that sounded faith-filled, like, "Praise God! It is wonderful to be in the house of the Lord. Glory,

Hallelujah!" You could never show that you were upset or that anything bad was happening at home.

There was also this unspoken rule: If you responded to an altar call and fell to the ground, that one touch at the altar would be enough. You were expected to get up and be "fixed." While some people did have radical transformations at the altar and were never the same again, many went back to their pews still riddled with anxiety, fear, and troubled minds—bound to their addictions. There was such an emphasis on the one-touch encounter that many pastors neglected to teach about the long-term sanctification process that happens as we grow in our faith in Jesus and develop our relationship with the Holy Spirit.

My mum was hungry to learn, and she believed in her heart that Jesus could heal her wounds. Because of her conviction, she made it her mission to discover what the Word of God said about her situation. She devoured the Scriptures, spent countless hours praying, and was delivered from the pain and anguish of her past. She recalls being schooled by the Holy Spirit in the secret place. My mum, who could hardly speak English, learned about the things of God because she positioned herself to do the work with the Holy Spirit.

When she attended Bible studies and church meetings, she would go home and apply everything she learned. She would read the Word and lock herself in her prayer closet until she felt a shift in her spirit, heart, and mind. She was relentless in her pursuit of the Holy Spirit. Every time the Enemy came to accuse her mind, she learned to take every thought captive and make it obedient to Christ according to 2 Corinthians 10:5. It was not an easy road, and she stumbled along the way, but my mum went from being a tormented, angry person who was broken from the inside out to a loving, caring prayer warrior who moved in power when she prayed. She chose to live from love and not strive to be loved. "For God so loved the world that He gave His only begotten Son, that whosoever believes in Him should not perish but have everlasting life" (John 3:16 NKJV). Because she had a revelation of His love, she could apply the truths of God's Word in her everyday life. And she is still that woman today.

Through the sanctification process in the school of the Holy Spirit and by being active in her church community, her life has been transformed, and I praise God that she did the work to become the woman God created her to be. I thank God that she did not give up. She has been faithfully walking with the Lord for nearly sixty years. I believe that because she chose to break the generational patterns of thinking and the effects of abuse, she made a way for me to find freedom from the trauma that I would later experience.

I often watched her lock herself away and cry out to God for mercy and healing. I remember sitting outside her closet door, weeping, as I could feel the presence of God coming from that room. She had no other option but Jesus. She didn't know who to turn to, but she found the friendship of the Holy Spirit—her Divine Counselor who would guide her into all truth. She would pray in her heavenly language (tongues) for hours and come out having received revelation straight from heaven that would give her strategy for that day and the next.

She taught me how to lean into discomfort and allow the Holy Spirit to heal those dark places so that I could come out on the other side victorious. I am so grateful for the path she forged for me to walk on. She chose not to numb her pain with lesser things or avoid going to the deep places that would require growth. The result was true freedom—a freedom that she walks in with full authority. When we are willing to do the work with the Holy Spirit, we allow Him not only to bring freedom to our lives but to the generations that come after us.

My mum did not have anyone to look up to in her family. Since she was the first person to be born again in her family, it was up to her to be the change for future generations. Maybe you didn't have a mom like I did or someone who could be an example for you, and that's okay. My mum pioneered a new way with the Holy Spirit by her side, and you can too. This is why it is necessary for the church to understand that we are all being sanctified in our walk with Jesus. Through God's Word, He is renewing our minds to be transformed into the likeness of Jesus Christ. He is truth, so when His truth is living inside us, we have the hope that we can be free, healed, and made whole. However, to say that it happens with one prayer and one touch from God is reckless and dangerous. I believe this mindset has contributed to the mismanagement of people's healing journeys and is one of the reasons we have a generation that is struggling to live in the freedom that Christ died to give us.

OUR DIVINE COUNSELOR

As we journey through these pages, I believe you will learn about and experience freedom as you develop a relationship with Jesus through the person of the Holy Spirit, your Divine Counselor. Please don't get me wrong. Receiving counsel is an important part of our healing process. I want to make you aware, however, that you have access to a superior counselor in the Holy Spirit, available 24/7, each and every day. He can guide you in *all* truth and my hope is that I can introduce you to Him and reveal Him as a person. Once you truly know, understand, and see the Holy Spirit as a person, you will want nothing more than to engage with Him, sit in His presence, and ultimately allow Him to transform your entire life.

You have access to a superior counselor in the Holy Spirit, available 24/7, each and every day.

He is the One who knows you better than you know yourself and who has seen every detail of your life—the good, the bad, and the ugly. He is the One who will bring healing to the darkest places if you allow the counsel of God to guide you. It takes practice to hear and recognize His voice, but the more you know Him, the more you can trust Him, obey Him, and walk in greater freedom, which will lead to greater authority. I know this for certain because not only is my mum a completely different person than when she was younger, but I am as well.

I have been a pastor for more than thirty years now, and I have witnessed countless people find true release from strongholds and bondage—freedom they could not achieve by just talking through their problems. You will read some of their stories in this book. The supernatural power of the Holy Spirit has delivered us and given us a new life—one of peace and contentment. It is not a life of perfection or one free from trouble, but one that is steadfast, complete with a sound mind and strong heart!

Those who have moved too far on the pendulum swing and cut God out of the equation entirely instead of allowing the counsel of Holy Spirit to bring healing have built a narrative that is so intertwined with worldly views that freedom and healing feel impossible with God. Perhaps many have completely neglected the Holy Spirit because they don't believe He has the power to heal or give wise counsel. Maybe some have become content with life as they know it, resolved to cope the best they know how, receive good advice, and read self-help books instead of seeking "the Helper." While none of this is inherently bad, all of it, without the demonstration of the supernatural power of God, can be only a temporary fix.

As Christians, we need to remember that there is nothing our God is not capable of. We don't get to tell God what He can and can't do. He is God, and we are not. We were never meant to lower our theology of God to fit with our earthly experience. Just because you are not experiencing healing right now does not mean that God cannot heal you. Just because you haven't received an answer to a prayer you have been praying doesn't change the fact that with God all things are possible.

When your belief system does not line up with Scripture and you live life consumed by the problem rather than looking toward the One with the solution, you will miss out on the healing you desire. There is a powerful maturing that happens to your faith when you stay faithful to the promises of God, even when you can't see or feel Him working. As the church, when we fail to teach people how to be strong and equip them to be courageous while enduring hardships, we unknowingly teach a generation to become weak, spiritually irresponsible, and unaccountable for their actions. We teach them to make excuses for their behavior instead of providing the tools to help them rise above the mess they are in. For the sake of those we have been entrusted to lead, as well as for the next generation, this has to change.

I have a deep desire to see believers use wisdom and gain understanding for the times we live in, and I believe this generation is rising up to access their heavenly Father and live in the Word of God. "For the word of God is alive and active. Sharper than any double-edged sword, it penetrates even to dividing soul and spirit, joints and marrow; it judges the thoughts and attitudes of the heart" (Hebrews 4:12). This is why the Bible says, "Keep your heart with all diligence, for out of it spring the issues of life" (Proverbs 4:23 NKJV). We must guard our hearts in this battle that rages for our attention, devotion, and conviction. It's time for us, as Christians, to take control of the pendulum swing by receiving a fresh revelation of who the Divine Counselor truly is in our lives.

As I am penning these words, I am tearing up because I want each one of you to experience the freedom that is available to you. My hope and prayer is that you will discover just how wonderful He is and how much He longs to be in relationship with you. He wants to walk and talk with you intimately through life's issues, guiding you into all truth so you can live a life that brings glory to God.

Would you take a moment to pray and ask the Holy Spirit to reveal Himself as you read through the pages of this book? Earnestly ask Him to bring wisdom and revelation to you and when He does, apply the tools that are given to you. I promise that when you make a conscious effort to seek Him, you will find Him in a new and fresh way. You will meet the person of the Holy Spirit, who longs to know you intimately and deeply and be with you more than you will ever understand.

PRAYER

Dear Jesus, my desire is to know You and Holy Spirit in a personal way. I ask You to reveal the Holy Spirit to me as the Divine Counselor as I journey through these pages. I pray that You draw me into close fellowship with the Holy Spirit so that our relationship will grow, and in turn, I will grow. I am hungry to know You in a deep and intimate way. I pray that as I learn more about You, I will discover the freedom that Jesus paid the price for me to encounter. In Your name I pray, amen.

CHAPTER 2

Do You Want to Be Well?

There are several moments in the Gospels where Jesus encounters a person and asks, "Do you want to be made well?" or "What do you want?" Jesus knew what they needed, but He wanted to hear from them what they wanted. In order to experience transformation in our lives, we have to desire change, and no one can do the work for us. Jesus longs for us to admit to Him what we need, but sometimes we want Him to do all the work for us. Jesus longs to be invited into our stories, but until we humble ourselves and admit that we need help, nothing will ever change. We will remain in the same exhausting cycles that only serve to keep us sick and stuck. When we are willing to come to the end of ourselves and admit that the ways we have tried to cope don't work, then we move from playing the victims in our stories to discovering the victory we have in Christ. If we want to walk in the fullness that He has for us, then we need to ask ourselves the question: *Do I* want *to get well? And if so, Jesus, would You help me?*

We must all come to this place of decision. Many people may think that all the work to be done in our lives happens at salvation, but we are not a finished work at salvation. According to Scripture, we are being transformed into the image of God through the sanctification process. Salvation is just the entrance to this new life with Christ. We must then learn to grow in our walk with God and be conformed to the image of Jesus through the power of the Holy Spirit. The Bible says, "And we all, with unveiled face, *continually* seeing as in a mirror the glory of the Lord, are *progressively* being transformed into His image from [one degree of] glory to [even more] glory, which comes from the Lord, [who is] the Spirit" (2 Corinthians 3:18 AMP). This means we are always changing and growing! The good news is that the apostle Paul said, "I am sure of this, that he who started a good work in you will carry it on to completion until the day of Christ Jesus" (Philippians 1:6 CSB).

The *inner man* refers to the spiritual aspect of a person, which is different from the physical, outer man. It represents the core of a person's being—including their spirit, soul, and mind—where God's Spirit dwells and works. The inner man is where spiritual transformation, renewal, and communion with God occur. Spiritual formation is the ongoing process of being transformed into the image of Christ by the Holy Spirit through spiritual disciplines like prayer, worship, reading the Word, and engaging with community—where we put into practice what we are learning. It's a progressive change over time as we keep moving forward in the right direction with the Holy Spirit leading us into all truth.

We need to be saturated in His truth, especially on the days when our inner turmoil wants to win. But the wounds of our past have a way of wreaking havoc in our lives and relationships when they are left unaddressed. If we are not diligent in keeping the Enemy's lies from penetrating our hearts, our souls will continue to be at unrest. Many of us are suppressing or ignoring the underlying issues in our lives, however, which only causes anger, resentment, and torment to ravage our inner man.

Mental health issues are at an all-time high, even within the church. While it is encouraging that these struggles have been destigmatized, allowing people to admit when they are not okay, a troubling trend has emerged. The diagnoses meant to offer clarity and explain our struggles are becoming increasingly embraced as part of our identity. By labeling ourselves with these diagnoses, we turn them into something concrete that justifies our behaviors and attitudes. As a result, we begin to believe that healing is not possible because "this is just who I am."

I've heard people claim mental struggles and disorders as the core of who they are: "my anxiety," "my depression," "my OCD," "my bipolar," and the list goes on. Instead of embarking on the journey of healing, we often remain "not okay," and develop coping mechanisms rather than bring our pain to the One who knows us better than we know ourselves. We were never meant to live in dysfunction or be defined by the issues we face.

Defining ourselves according to any broken area in our lives can be dangerous. If you have been diagnosed with a mental illness by a licensed clinician, I am not saying your problems are not valid and can be ignored. I am saying that we get to choose how to allow God to move in our lives. When we label ourselves as the problem, we sometimes remove ourselves from the responsibility to do the work that is required to experience authentic freedom, and we end up claiming ownership over a place the Word of God has already declared we have power and authority over. We can speak death over ourselves by constantly telling ourselves who we are, and the Bible says, "As [a man] thinks in his heart, so is he" (Proverbs 23:7 NKJV). Our words and our thoughts are incredibly powerful. They hold power: "The tongue has the power of life and death, and those who love it will eat its fruit" (18:21). Christ died to set us free from anxiety and fear; therefore, we do not need to own them as part of our identity.

All of us go through anxious times—some more than others. I am not denying that it can be debilitating, but at the core of anxiety is fear, and we must get to the root of that fear, not just cope and live with anxiety. Doing the work takes time and intentionality. We will have to die to ourselves, which does not feel good in the process. This is why many stay stuck in victim mentalities and are never able to fully heal. They make excuses and never get to the root because the work of healing can often feel more painful than the wound itself.

> The work of healing can often feel more painful than the wound itself.

In Christ we were made a new creation; the old is gone and the new has come (2 Corinthians 5:17). The sad reality, though, is that so many of us are carrying our dead corpses on our backs as we try to live this new life as followers of Christ. We don't realize the baggage we are carrying, and we end up blaming it on other people instead of bringing it to Jesus. We must allow the Holy Spirit to reveal the truth and give us the tools we need to truly heal. Wounds are often open and bleeding, and if left unattended, they can become infected and may result in death. Scars, however, are wounds that have healed. They tell a story of what happened—but also what has now been healed. Jesus wants to turn your wounds into scars, and the only way He can do this is if we are honest and show Him where we are bleeding. James

5:16 says, "Therefore confess your sins to each other and pray for each other so that you may be healed." Confession, prayer, and faith are essential to healing the wounds of our past.

BLAMING VS. TAKING RESPONSIBILITY

I asked a close friend of mine, a licensed counselor, what patterns she's noticed over the years in those she had counseled. I asked what she thought the difference was between those who have been successful in overcoming their issues and those who became stuck and did not change. She said the reason so many never truly heal is because they either refuse to admit that they are unwell or deny that the problem exists with them. They blame others and are unwilling to take responsibility for their actions in the process. They want the counselor to do the work for them, hoping that just talking about it will cause the issues in their life to shift.

One of the biggest obstacles to healing is that people struggle to acknowledge they are sick. They often deflect and say things like, "Other people say that I am like this or that." But when asked directly if there is any truth in those statements, they respond, "Oh no, I am not like that at all," ignoring the fact that sometimes the problem lies within them but they don't want to confront it in counseling.

No one likes the thought of being sick. But what do we do when we are physically ill? We reach for remedies that will help us feel back to normal as quickly as possible. In a similar way, God does not desire that any of us stay spiritually sick. He reveals so He can heal. Sometimes the shame is so deep that the thought of bringing it to light feels worse than the transgression done to us. We need to be vulnerable and transparent when looking inward and allow the Holy Spirit to help reveal what we sometimes find hard to articulate. Until we bring everything that is hidden into the light, we forfeit the process that is necessary for our full healing. We can choose to resist the Holy Spirit when He prompts us to change, or we can yield to His still, small voice; surrender to His will instead of our own; and allow Him to make us well.

I once heard a story from a doctor of psychology who shared about his wife who went to a seminar while she was battling cancer. The seminar featured discussions across various aspects of psychology, trauma, mental health, and emotional health. Since she had suffered from a great deal of trauma as a child, she decided to attend. After the seminar ended, she struck up a conversation with the seminar leader.

The man asked her an interesting question after she shared about her struggle with cancer. He asked, "How much responsibility do you want for this?" At first, she was offended and responded, "I didn't do this to myself. It's not my fault. I have cancer." He looked at her and said, "I didn't ask you about blame. I will ask the question again. How much responsibility do you want for this situation in your life?" She answered, "I want 100 percent responsibility." He went on to explain that when you blame others for your problems, you become the victim, and you can't change. The hallmark of self-defeating behavior is blaming others for the problems in your life. He said responsibility is *your ability to respond* to any given situation in your life. The only way to overcome it is to stop playing the blame game and ask yourself: *What is my responsibility in this?*

Please listen to me, friend. The issue you are facing may not be your fault. It may be something someone did to you, and I am not diminishing that pain. I know it's real. But even though it may not be your fault, it has become your problem. And with the help of the Holy Spirit, it's your responsibility to take ownership so you can overcome. Blaming someone else will only keep you in bondage and prohibit you from moving into freedom.

For years I blamed everyone else for my issues. While what I went through was not fair or okay, I couldn't change what had happened. I had to face the reality that the only way forward was changing how I responded. I could either keep holding unforgiveness and become sicker, or I could choose to forgive and receive healing. We all have a choice to either react or respond when things happen to us. For many years I chose to react because it fed my flesh and made me feel better, but in reality I was not getting any healthier. I was getting worse because I lived in a constant state of blame and refused to take responsibility for myself.

With the help of the Holy Spirit, it's your responsibility to take ownership so you can overcome.

Blame is defined as shifting responsibility to someone else for a fault or wrong that has been done. We blame others even when it's something small. Blame may sound like, "That person made me late because they took too long to get ready," or "She made me feel guilty when she said . . . ," or "They pressured me to decide. I had no choice in the matter," or "I'm depressed because of the way I was raised," or "He made me explode with rage when he triggered me by doing that thing he knows I hate."

Blaming others may be the most natural reaction in the

moment, but it ultimately leads to destructive emotions such as resentment, anger, and hatred. We often blame others for our negative behavior instead of taking responsibility for our response when unfair things happen to us. The reason we do this is because blame takes us off the hook of feeling guilty and makes us feel better temporarily. It is also a defense mechanism. When we feel attacked, we get defensive.

Failing to hold ourselves accountable for the consequences of our own behaviors, thoughts, feelings, and actions keeps us stuck in the trap of thinking we have minimal flaws or areas that need growth. Shifting blame onto others is simply a refusal to take ownership in how we contributed to our problems. It's the easy way out. When we feel triggered by something, who do we blame? The other person! But your triggers are not someone else's responsibility. Only you can deal with and face the root issues in your own life. This refusal to accept responsibility denies us control of a given situation. It leaves us powerless and ultimately stunts our personal and spiritual growth. In fact, when we choose to ignore any sign, big or small, regarding the displacement of blame, we can even find ourselves pushing away those who are coming from a place of support.

If we want to live the life of freedom that Christ died to give us, we can't stay in a perpetual cycle of blame. When we address the situation with the attention it deserves, it's much easier to read our own emotions and see the reason behind the underlying issue. Responsibility is required, not optional. What is your response when something terrible happens? Is it blame or do you see it as an opportunity to allow God to come in and heal the broken places of your heart? I once heard a therapist say that not every struggle in life is trauma and not every workplace is toxic.

I would add, the Enemy is not always attacking you. Life is hard at times, and we need to learn how to do hard things. We are stronger than we realize because of God's power that is at work within us. If we allow God to teach us how to overcome, He will. The question is: Will you let Him?

The truth is, we grow stronger when there is resistance. Pain is inevitable. But instead of dodging it, we have to be able to face it head-on if we are ever going to step into what God has purposed for our lives. Much like resistance training helps build our physical muscles, as we endure time under tension in life, our spiritual muscles grow stronger as well. You must lift heavy things for your muscles to grow. And if you want to keep growing in strength, the weight you lift must increase. You can't stay stagnant and stuck and expect growth. We will never grow the muscles needed for longevity if we try to avoid the hard things.

We must push through the pain barrier to grow in strength. Paul talked about these challenging life situations, reminding us of how the Lord responds to us in these moments: "But he said to me, 'My grace is sufficient for you, for my power is made perfect in weakness.' Therefore, I will boast all the more gladly about my weaknesses, so that Christ's power may rest on me. That is why, for Christ's sake, I delight in weaknesses, in insults, in hardships, in persecutions, in difficulties. For when I am weak, then I am strong" (2 Corinthians 12:9–10).

Jesus ultimately covers our lack of natural strength with His supernatural power, but we must lean into the temporary discomfort and pain to build spiritual muscle maturity. When we decide to quit, give up, and lie down, we become weaker in the long run. The saying "no pain, no gain" is so true when it comes to facing our issues. It may feel uncomfortable at first, but you have a choice: Either live with chronic pain for the rest of your life or face discomfort for a short period of time in exchange for freedom for the rest of your life. You get to choose—and life is all about choices.

THE MAN AT THE POOL OF BETHESDA

This reminds me of the story in the Gospel of John about a man who was paralyzed for thirty-eight years. When asked if he wanted to be well, the paralyzed man blamed those around him for his lack of healing. Even though he was physically healed by the power of Jesus, he didn't receive full healing from his spiritual illness.

> When Jesus saw him lying there and learned that he had been in this condition for a long time, He asked him, "Do you want to get well?"
>
> "Sir," the invalid replied, "I have no one to help me into the pool when the water is stirred. While I am trying to get in, someone else goes down ahead of me."
>
> Then Jesus said to him, "Get up! Pick up your mat and walk." At once the man was cured; he picked up his mat and walked. (John 5:6–9)

Much like the people of the world today who turn to superstitions, potions, lotions, crazy rituals, or self-help books to find healing, many during this time in history believed the Pool of Bethesda had healing powers. People believed that an angel came and stirred the waters. According to local tradition, the first person in the water after it was stirred would be healed. Nowhere in Scripture do we find this to be a fact. Rather, it was a superstition of the day.

The Bible says that Jesus learned of this man's condition—not because someone told Him, but through the Spirit of God, who led Him to the man and revealed the details to Him. When Jesus arrived at the pool where many needed healing, He chose this one man and asked Him a question: "Do you want to be well?" It seems like an odd question to ask someone who is clearly disabled and in need of help. Jesus was asking because being healed would require this man to have to take responsibility and get to work.

I love what William Barclay said about this question:

> It was not so foolish a question as it may sound. The man had waited for thirty-eight years, and it might well have been that hope had died and left behind a passive and dull despair. In his heart of hearts, the man might be well content to remain an invalid for, if he were cured, he would have all the burden of making a living. He might have grown accustomed to his disability, being able to leave the working and the worrying to someone else. But his response was immediate. He wanted to be healed, though he did not see how he ever could be since no one was there to help him. The first essential towards receiving the power of Jesus is to have an intense desire for it. Jesus says: "Do you really want to be changed?" If in our inmost hearts we are well content to stay as we are, there can be no change for us.[1]

I remember when I suffered with an eating disorder, I would often sense the Holy Spirit asking me that question during the twenty years that I walked in bondage to this addiction. My answer for so long was no. I may not have said it out loud but deep down in my heart, I did not want to get well. I just wanted sympathy for my pain. I got locked into being the victim of my circumstances because others felt sorry for me and for what had been done to me. It gave me an excuse not to move on with my life and justification to stay stuck in the cycle of pain. My issue had become such a source of comfort that I didn't even realize it had become my identity and my friend.

In a weird way, this sickness actually fueled the deficit in me that needed filling. For example, the more I lost weight, the more I found myself being affirmed by others for the way I looked. It was like a drug. Receiving compliments and feeling loved by others became my drug of choice. So even though my mind was in complete agreement with the need to heal, deep down in my heart, I was not ready to give up what brought me a sense of comfort. At least, not just yet. I didn't want to get well because healing meant doing the hard work of confronting the root issue in my heart, and that felt more overwhelming and even more painful than the wound itself.

How many times do we choose comfort over confronting the issue because the Enemy has convinced us that confronting it will hurt more? He tempts us to stay bound by our issues and stuck in endless cycles of struggles, deceiving us into thinking it is someone else's problem to fix rather than our own. I kept justifying why I did what I did, instead of asking the Holy Spirit how to overcome. My breakthrough finally came when I chose to be done with the continual suffering that resulted from my decision to keep it hidden and refusal to admit that I needed help. I had to choose to let go and allow Jesus to heal my brokenness so I could get well, and that required something from me: a yielding, a surrendering, and a decision to stop blaming and start taking the responsibility that I needed to take.

And I did. I yielded my heart, surrendered my will, and said, "Father, forgive me for wanting to put up with this suffering instead of surrendering to Your lordship. I'm tired of living like this. I want to be well, and I'm willing to do the work—with You. I'll do whatever it takes, as long as You're leading me." I had to forgive the person who hurt me deeply. I had to take responsibility, knowing that even though what had been done to me was not my fault, I could no longer blame anyone else for being bound. As soon as I did that, Jesus healed me. He delivered me from the eating disorder supernaturally in a moment, and then I had to walk out my freedom by renewing my mind with His Word.

He filled the areas where I needed affirmation with His love. He began to tell me what He loved about me, and it filled the void that I was so busy trying to fill for all those years. He taught me how to speak life over myself every time the Enemy would whisper a lie. I would take those thoughts captive and make them obedient to what Jesus said about me. Each time the Enemy tempted me to fall back into old habits, I would declare God's Word and speak truth over my mind and heart. I also made myself accountable to people I trusted. When I felt like I was slipping into bad patterns, I would confess my thoughts and bring them into the light, which disabled the Enemy's stronghold over me. Over time, I was able to walk freely out of the bondage that had held me captive for twenty years.

As we pick back up in John 5, we see Jesus asked the man, "Do you want to get well?" (v. 6). Immediately, the man replied with blame. He said, "I have no one to help me into the pool when the water is stirred. While I am trying to get in, someone else goes down ahead of me" (v. 7).

This man's response to Jesus includes limitations, excuses for why he cannot be healed, blame against other people who are healed, and justifications for why he cannot get well. I believe Jesus is standing before us this very moment, asking us the same question: Do you want to be well?

I love what Terry Storch says about this:

> This is our God, this is our Savior, this is the Creator of the universe and He stands before us in this very moment offering the same to us. What is our response, are we going to list all the reason why we are stuck? Are we going to walk through our past, our baggage, our issues, and all our situations that we are justifying our mindset and our inaction? Jesus said, "Would you like to get well?"
>
> God stands ready to do infinitely more than we can hope, dream, or imagine. Jesus is asking us if we would like to get well. Do we desire to be healed? If so, stand up, pick up your mat, and walk. What often seems impossible in our lives just needs the appropriate faith and focus on Jesus.[2]

What mindsets are making you paralyzed and keeping you sick? And the question we need to ask ourselves is: Do we want to get well? We must desire change, no matter the cost, before we can experience true healing.

I find this passage of Scripture interesting because Jesus didn't even address the man's excuses. He went right to the solution. Jesus simply said, "Get up! Pick up your mat and walk" (John 5:8). The man made the effort to obey Jesus' command, despite the questions I'm sure were running through his mind. Miraculously, the man was healed! But when the Pharisees saw him carrying his mat on the Sabbath, which was against rabbinic law, he escaped by saying that Jesus made him do it. He blamed Jesus so that he wouldn't get into trouble with the Pharisees (vv. 9–15).

Although his outer body experienced a healing, his inner man had not changed. According to the text, there was absolutely no honor or gratitude on this man's part. The saddest part of the whole story is that the miracle was completely overlooked—the man was healed, yet the religious leaders were focused on a broken law. Later, Jesus found this man and saw that he still had no change of heart after being healed. The man didn't share with the Pharisees the good news about his healing. He just blamed Jesus for making him take up his mat. Jesus said to him, "Stop sinning, or something worse may happen to you" (v. 14). He wasn't warning that more physical sickness would come, but that his spiritual condition would be far worse if he died without repentance.

God is more interested in your faith being made well than your physical body being healed. What good is it to get partial healing and not *full* healing? This is the danger we face when we harden our hearts toward God in the process of our healing. When we choose to take responsibility for our actions and tell the truth, instead of shifting blame out of fear of what others might think, we've already fought half the battle. The comforting truth in this process is that the Holy Spirit will never ask us to do the work alone. He wants to give us the keys of the kingdom that will help deliver us from the strongholds in our lives, and He is there to show us how to do that.

BOLD FAITH REQUIRES ACTION

You can decide, today, to do whatever it takes to pursue healing from the ultimate Healer, Jesus Christ, just like the woman in Mark 5 who came to the end of herself and decided to pursue healing, no matter the cost.

> A large crowd followed and pressed around him. And a woman was there who had been subject to bleeding for twelve years. She had suffered a great deal under the care of many doctors and had spent all she had, yet instead of getting better she grew worse. When she heard about Jesus, she came up behind him in the crowd and touched His cloak, because she thought, "If I just touch his clothes, I will be healed." Immediately her bleeding stopped and she felt in her body that she was freed from her suffering.
>
> At once Jesus realized that power had gone out from him. He turned around in the crowd and asked, "Who touched my clothes?"
>
> "You see the people crowding against you," his disciples answered, "and yet you can ask, 'Who touched me?'" But Jesus kept looking around to see who had done it. Then the woman, knowing what had happened to her, came and fell at his feet and, trembling with fear, told him the whole truth. He said to her, "Daughter, your faith has healed you. Go in peace and be freed from your suffering." (Mark 5:24–34)

The woman in this passage of Scripture has no name, but she is identified by her issue. We know her as "the woman with the issue of blood." How many times do we stereotype people and label them by their issue, instead of taking the time to get to know who they truly are? Society is constantly putting labels on people—"the crazy one," "the divorced one," "the abused one," "the promiscuous one," or "the mean one." We have all been subjected to stereotypes because of unfortunate circumstances, but that is not who we are. That's simply part of our story, a reflection of what's been done to us, not what defines us.

This woman had been *subject to* bleeding for twelve years. She suffered a great deal physically, emotionally, and spiritually. She tried everything. She went to every doctor and spent all she had on tonics, potions, and any other medication available to her. I'm sure many of the things she tried were just superstitions, but there's no doubt she tried them all because she was desperate. The Bible says that, despite all her efforts, she didn't get better. She only grew worse. This issue not only affected her health, it also rendered her unclean to her community. Having an issue like this during biblical times meant she was cut off from others and forbidden from worshiping in the temple. Her issue impacted her entire life.

As we study this story a little deeper, we find that the phrase *subject to* means something is dependent on, conditional upon, or likely to be affected by something else. It can also mean being exposed or open to something or experiencing something unpleasant. What are you subject to? What issues do *you* have? What issue in your life has defined who you are to the people around you and maybe even to yourself? You may not be physically hemorrhaging like this woman, but are you emotionally hemorrhaging from pain and bleeding out in your soul? *Hemorrhaging* is a medical term for excessive bleeding from a damaged blood vessel or organ. It can be internal or external, and if serious, it can be life-threatening.

This woman suffered from more than just a physical ailment. While her condition was rooted in being physically unwell, her issues ran much deeper. With no recorded name in Scripture, she would have been marginalized, isolated, invisible, embarrassed, weak, lifeless, alone, stereotyped, ceremonially unclean, unwanted by men, unwanted by the female community, unwelcome to worship with others, and most likely unmarried. If she had been married, he likely left her. She would've been completely broke, having spent everything on doctors in vain attempts to find a cure. The more money she spent and the harder she tried superstitious remedies, the worse her condition grew. Year after year, disappointment after disappointment, she was hopeless. She had exhausted all natural options, but she heard about Jesus and resolved to give it one last shot. She chose to do something bold!

Her issue was so embarrassing that to admit it openly in a crowd was something society wouldn't allow her to do. She was ceremonially unclean, which meant anything she touched also became unclean. The stakes were high, and she was about to risk everything. She could have made excuses based on what society deemed appropriate behavior, yet she didn't let other people's opinions stop her from taking personal responsibility for her healing. She made the decision to crawl on the ground up to Jesus—probably at the risk of being stepped on and crushed as the crowds surrounded Him. She couldn't go any lower than how she was approaching Jesus.

Completely humiliated and terrified, she reached out in faith and tried to touch Him in secrecy. She thought, *If only I could touch the hem of His garment, I will be healed!* This is how this woman received her healing! It cost her. It cost her faith, embarrassment, grit, trust, and a resolve to not give up. Healing has a cost. But when we decide to do *whatever* it takes to touch Jesus, no matter the cost, that is when we can be made whole. We must first come to the end of ourselves so that Jesus can start doing the work that only He is empowered to do in our lives!

WHAT ARE YOU THINKING?

I love how Mark told us that this woman thought to herself. What are your thoughts telling you? Are you rationalizing all the reasons why you shouldn't do what is in your heart to do? Are you afraid that if you put yourself out there, nothing will happen? Or is your faith nonexistent, paralyzing you and keeping you stuck in your issue like the paralytic man we read about in John 5?

In Romans, Paul reminded us that our "faith comes by hearing, and hearing by the word of God" (10:17 NKJV). When we speak death over our lives, we diminish the faith realm and stay stuck in our pain. However, when our thinking shifts—when we believe the truth of God's Word over our feelings—our faith begins to increase. And as our faith increases, we can courageously step out, even when we feel afraid. Faith not only moves us, but it also moves the heart of God. Ultimately, faith makes us brave! Being brave is not the absence of fear. Rather, it is overcoming fear and acting in spite of it.

Scripture says that "because she thought, 'If I just touch his clothes, I will be healed,'" her bleeding stopped immediately (Mark 5:28–29). Scripture also says that "she felt in her body that she was freed from her suffering" (v. 29). It was her faith—it was first a thought and then activated by her actions—that propelled her to take a step, reach out, and touch Jesus. This is ultimately what caught Jesus' attention. He immediately realized that someone had touched Him on purpose. This woman drew virtue out of Him. That's what faith does when we step out of our comfort zone and decide to receive from Jesus' healing power. So many of us are waiting for Jesus to come to us, but we can go to Him! No matter what issue you're facing, you can reach out and touch Him by faith.

This is a paradigm shift for some of us who have been taught that the Bible is only a story *about* Jesus. But the truth is, the Bible is also a book of encounters *with* Jesus that set a precedent to build our faith and give us a guide for how to pursue our own healing. The stories we read are designed to build our faith to the point where we can say, "If it happened for them, it can also happen for me." So, friend, I'll ask you again. What are you thinking about? Your thought life will determine whether you stay a prisoner to your circumstances or step into the breakthrough you've been longing for.

> Your thought life will determine whether you stay a prisoner to your circumstances or step into the breakthrough you've been longing for.

The Bible says that as soon as power left Jesus, He stopped and asked, "Who touched my clothes?" (v. 30). No one responded, and yet Jesus wouldn't take silence as an answer. He kept looking around the crowd until the person who touched Him revealed herself. He didn't move on. I can imagine the hush that fell over the crowd as everyone's eyes darted back and forth, wondering who it was. A heavy silence sweeping through the air—thick and tense, the kind where you could hear a pin drop.

Her heart was probably beating a million miles a minute,

because right then she had a choice to come clean with her confession. It could have come at a high price. She risked judgment, mockery, and screaming from the people around her. They could have accused her of making them unclean. Yet Jesus waited. He was not in a hurry. We don't know how long He waited, but when you are faced with choosing whether to be vulnerable or not, two minutes can feel like an eternity. With fear and trembling, this woman stepped forward and told Jesus the whole truth.

She was ready to give it all up! Confession in this crowd would have been humiliating and terrifying, yet as soon as she confessed the whole truth to Jesus, the fear and trembling left her. Jesus stepped in and declared something profound to her. Where she had once been known as "the woman with the issue," Jesus renamed her. He called her daughter! Not only did He immediately heal her, but He also redefined her identity in society and established her position as daughter. He said to her, "Your faith has healed you. Go in peace and be freed from your suffering" (v. 34). She was healed physically *and* delivered emotionally from shame. Immediately. Jesus confirmed what she had thought: Her faith was stronger than her fear.

When He called her daughter, He sealed her position in Christ (Himself). He changed her identity and removed the labels from her life. This is exactly what Jesus wants to do for us, but we must first be brutally honest about where we are. I hope this encourages you, that no matter how unworthy you feel or how many times you have believed the lie that Jesus doesn't care about your issue—He still wants you to come to Him even if you do it scared. You can choose to stay broken, ashamed, and defined by your issue or you can step into your identity as His child. Jesus affirmed her—not only to herself but also to the crowd. She was no longer defined as the woman with the issue. She left that encounter with Jesus healed in her body, freed from her suffering, and knowing with full peace that she was God's *daughter*!

He gave her a name, *daughter*. This meant she had a position as an heir of God so she could live her life on purpose. The end of her suffering meant she could reenter society, build community, find love, and perhaps even have a family—something she may have longed for all those years living in isolation. Jesus made her whole. That is the goal for all of us as believers: that we would discover life and life abundantly just as Jesus promised!

Jesus assured us, "Peace I leave you, My peace I give you; not as the world gives, do I give to you. Let not your heart be troubled, nor fearful" (John 14:27 NASB). This supernatural peace, which comes as a fruit of the Spirit, is what the world is desperately searching for. The question Holy Spirit is asking is, "Do you want to be well?" He invites you into transformation. He is a gentleman who doesn't boss you into freedom. Rather, He invites you to be honest with Him. He invites you to partner with Him in the process of healing from wounds that you've been content to cover with a spiritual bandage, pretending they don't exist if you don't look too closely.

It's only when we are completely honest and vulnerable with Him that He can take our pain, suffering, and affliction, and turn it into lasting and genuine healing. He is the safest place to land, and He will never take advantage of you. He will always complete what He starts, and He most definitely will never leave you or forsake you. You get to choose if you want to stay sick on the inside or whether you'll finally come to the end of yourself and allow Jesus to come and heal you. Ask yourself: *Am I done making excuses? Am I ready to surrender to* whatever *God asks of me? Am I ready to step out in faith and touch Jesus? And do I* really *believe that He can make me well?*

PRAYER

Dear Jesus, I come to You with an open and honest heart to ask You to heal the areas that are hemorrhaging in my life. I give you access to reveal what needs to be healed. I choose to take responsibility if I have blamed others or chosen to sit in my pain instead of dealing with it and give You permission to come and heal those wounds. I repent for remaining a victim of what was done to me and for blaming others for my situation. Today, I choose to be honest about where I am. I believe You are the God who heals, so right now, Jesus, I ask You to heal those places that I have kept hidden from You and from others. Deliver me from my suffering in Jesus' name, amen.

CHAPTER 3

My Best Friend, Holy Spirit

When I was a little girl, I had an imaginary friend named Lisa. Every time I was sad or didn't understand why I felt the way I did, I would retreat to my bedroom, hop up on my bed, and pour my heart out to her. It really felt like she existed, and we would have full conversations. I never heard her voice respond, but I loved the way having this best friend made me feel. I could tell her anything, and I knew she wouldn't judge me. Growing up in an environment where my voice was rarely heard, respected, or valued, Lisa made me feel safe and secure. I would talk to her for hours about the struggles I was facing in my little world. But at the end of the day, I knew she wasn't real.

I was the youngest of four children growing up in the early '70s. You had to have your own fun, so I was often alone in my room or outside on my swing. We didn't have video games to play or technology to waste our time on. We had one television in the house with only five channels and programmed content. This meant most of my time was spent imagining, dreaming, and pondering, or conversing with Lisa.

At the core of how we are designed, I believe each one of us longs for a best friend we can call on at any time—someone who will give us wise advice when we are facing tough decisions, comfort us in times of deep pain or loss, and rejoice with us when life is sweet. Even though I grew out of having an imaginary friend, I went on to discover someone who would be better than any earthly best friend. He is better than siblings or imaginary friends. Let me introduce you to Him.

I was born into a Christian home. We grew up attending a Pentecostal Italian church. My mum was one of the Sunday school teachers and was deeply involved, which meant my siblings and I practically lived at church. In my young mind, I automatically assumed I was a Christian because our lives revolved around the church. I thought everyone who went to church was a Christian, and that only bad people went to hell.

Even though I was in church weekly, I didn't hear the gospel until I was eleven years old when a friend invited me to her church. I had never visited another church besides the little Italian church my parents attended. When we pulled into the parking lot, I was overwhelmed, to say the least. I had never seen anything like it. It looked like a university! My understanding of what a church should look like was shaped by our little Italian church in a downtown side alley that only fit around three hundred people. This church auditorium seated around four thousand. I could not believe my eyes, nor could I wait to open the doors and step inside.

I remember sitting in the middle section on the ground floor, right in front of the sound desk. I don't remember what the pastor spoke about that evening, but I do remember the moment he began his salvation appeal for those in the congregation to receive Christ as their Lord and Savior. My heart started racing. It felt like he was calling my name, and I remember sensing the inner voice of God inviting me to respond. He was drawing me to Himself with His unconditional love and unexplainable peace.

I didn't fully understand what was happening in that moment, but I felt heat all over my body—an undeniable pull to respond by walking down to the altar. I found myself quickly walking to the front of the church auditorium. I didn't know my short legs could move my body that fast. When I arrived at the altar, the pastor shared the gospel in a way I had never heard before. I realized in that moment that I was a sinner in need of a Savior, and His name was Jesus.

Even though I was only eleven years old, I understood I was guilty of the sin I had inherited, and this sin had separated me from God, my heavenly Father. I vividly remember the weight of sin lifting off my shoulders when I prayed that prayer of repentance. I could not stop crying tears of sorrow and simultaneously smiling with joy. I felt deep sorrow because I realized how much I had broken God's heart by living separately from Him, and overwhelming joy because Jesus Christ had died in my place—so now, I could be born again. I left the service that night literally jumping, leaping, and praising God. I went home and immediately told my mother and father what had happened at church. They were elated that I had received Jesus into my life!

I went to school the next day and felt completely different. Nothing had changed externally in my life. My circumstances at home were the same, my family was the same, school was the same, but everything inside me had supernaturally changed. I could not explain it with words, but there was joy, freedom, and hope I had never experienced before. I only told my best friend what had happened to me because I attended a Catholic private school, and I was a little cautious to tell people about my experience with Jesus. Most of my friends were Catholic by name but not in lifestyle, and they for sure would have labeled me "the weird one."

But I could hardly stand it! I had so much joy on the inside that I walked around school every day feeling like I was floating on cloud nine. That same week, a lady from the church where I was saved came over to review the foundations of Christianity with me. Her smile was wonderful, and she had the kindest eyes. She committed to come to my home every Monday for six weeks to teach me about my new relationship with Jesus.

She explained that it was the Holy Spirit who had drawn me to receive Jesus as my Lord and Savior. I began to wonder about the Holy Spirit and His role in my life. *How can I hear the voice of someone I have never met?* I wondered. She taught me that it is the purpose of the Holy Spirit to reveal Jesus to us and bring conviction to our hearts. The inner work of the Holy Spirit reveals the truth to us so we are able to recognize that we are sinners in need of a Savior.

> For all have sinned and fallen short of the glory of God. (Romans 3:23)

> For the wages of sin is death, but the gift of God is eternal life in Christ Jesus our Lord. (Romans 6:23)

Everyone who has repented of their sin, asked Jesus Christ to come make His home within them, and been born again has heard the inner voice of the Holy Spirit. You listened and then responded to His invitation. Therefore, you heard His voice. As a pastor, I've had many people who have been saved tell me that they can't hear God's voice. I gently remind them what Elaine told me: You *can* hear God's voice because you answered His question when you responded to receive Jesus as your Savior.

Looking back, I had no idea that my experience as an eleven-year-old girl would be a defining moment in my life. Little did I know, I was about to discover a relationship with the person of the Holy Spirit that would change my life and how I relate to God forever. I often reflect on the experience I had as a little girl, when faith in Jesus became personal to me. The week after I accepted Christ, my family went to our little Italian church, just as we had done my whole life. But something was different this time. I was different. I could not wait to get to church that week. I wanted more. I was hungry for more of God's Word, His presence, and His power. I sensed there was more to gain in Christ, but I wasn't sure how to access it.

At the end of the pastor's sermon, I found myself running down the aisle toward the altar as fast as I could. Most Sundays in this small Italian church, I was bored out of my mind, but this Sunday was different. I decided that I wanted to be baptized in the Holy Spirit after reading one of the lessons in the little booklet Elaine had given me. I didn't fully understand what it all meant. All I knew was that I wanted *more* of what I was experiencing. So, I ran to the front, raised my hands, in eager expectation for something more. The pastor, who didn't know what to do with me, just stared at me with a blank look on his face. Do you think that stopped me? Not one bit. Before I knew it, with my hands raised high and my eyes tightly shut, I was being baptized with the Holy Spirit, and I began to speak in tongues. Heat and electricity ran through my little body. My tongue began moving so fast, and sounds I had never heard before flowed out of my mouth. I couldn't stop it. It overwhelmed me in the best way.

I knew that this had to be a supernatural experience because I had heard my mum praying in tongues. I had so many memories of being at our house while my mum was in her room praying. She would pray in tongues while my brother and I made fun of her in the other room, talking gibberish and giggling to ourselves. But this time, it wasn't funny. I could not control what was happening. It was as if my tongue had been taken over by something—rather, *Someone*—and the words flowed out of my mouth with fluency and ease. I knew I had been marked by something powerful and beyond my natural understanding.

The best way to describe how it felt is that it was like a warm liquid running through my entire body. It was as if I was being wrapped up by God's presence, and I never wanted the moment to end. Tears streamed down my face as I realized that God was no longer distant but intimate. He was as close as I could ever feel to someone. I was safe, secure, and protected in His arms. It felt like I was having an out-of-body experience, yet I was very much present at the altar of my small home church.

I went home that Sunday completely different from how I had entered the church. The week before, when I invited Jesus into my heart, it felt like a weight had lifted off me and I was full of incomparable joy. But this week, I felt like I could take on the world! A boldness rose up in me that I couldn't describe. It was as if God Himself was present alongside me, and I was acutely aware of His presence within me. I felt His inner voice speaking to my heart. It made me want to tell everyone about Jesus and share the supernatural experience I had. I thought, *Everyone I know needs to encounter what I just encountered. My life has been impacted, and I am forever changed.*

Not everyone has the same experience as I did when being baptized in the Holy Spirit and that is completely okay. What I love about God is that He is personal and gentle. I have seen many people baptized over the years and it looks different for everyone. But one thing is evident: Something supernatural has taken place in each of their lives. Maybe you're reading this and thinking that what I'm sharing is a completely foreign concept. My hope is that it will ignite a spark and desire inside you to seek it for yourself. If so, in chapter 6 I dive deeper into being baptized in the Holy Spirit, teaching you from Scripture why this is so important in your personal walk with the Lord and how you can experience it. I promise you it will be worth it.

I have connected with many people over the past decade who have told me about their *religious* experience but not about their *personal* relationship with the Lord. Sometimes, church traditions, even with the best intentions, can get in the way of us experiencing the fullness of God's nature. For example, one of my friends grew up in a conservative church that didn't have musical instruments and prohibited women from pastoring or preaching. While the pastor taught God's Word diligently, my friend never experienced revelation. There was no illumination that led to transformation. Her religious experience was devoid of the life-changing power of the Holy Spirit.

Now, after having experienced a church that prioritizes pursuing God's presence and biblical revelation, she has words to articulate the struggles she encountered growing up. The legalistic rules and regulations demanded just enough to keep her from going to hell. She felt she had to endure the many trials in life on her own. She kept secrets hidden in her heart because she had limited knowledge of how to access heavenly help. She had not been taught that she carried power to overcome the issues of life she faced, as well as the trauma of toxic past relationships. In her mind, God didn't help with those things—because all He wanted was for us to be good girls and boys and follow His law.

When she walked into a church service at The Belonging Co, everything changed. She was now an adult and had years of incorrect theology to confront. I remember her telling me, "I didn't know how to articulate it then, but I could sense something was different. People were not performing for God; they were engaging with God on a personal level. This was intimate, unlike anything I'd ever experienced."[1] She could sense the tangible presence of God for the first time. It made her feel safe and left her wanting more. Little did she know the Holy Spirit, who she had been afraid of and confused by, was about to become her very best friend. Ultimately, in His divine counsel, He healed the deepest wounds in her heart that had gone untouched for years. Today she is still walking out her life alongside the Holy Spirit in complete freedom!

When I received my prayer language, I didn't just speak in tongues. My life was changed and I discovered a person who I could deeply connect with. Have you ever spent time with a close friend and found yourselves so engaged in conversation that hours passed without you even realizing it? I talked to Him just as I would talk to a friend sitting right across from me. Except, He is a friend who can speak directly to my heart like no person can. I had a real and accessible relationship with Him. He illuminated the Scriptures to me in a profound way. I remember reading God's Word and feeling like the passage came alive in front of me. It made sense to me! I would find myself speaking out revelations that felt so above my natural understanding.

When I needed advice about something that was concerning me, instead of worrying about it like I used to, I would pick up the Bible and He would answer the very cry of my heart through a Scripture verse. It felt as though He was in my bedroom, sitting at the end of the bed, longing to have conversations with me. I felt His nearness in my lowest moments and His presence caused me to weep tears of joy and gratitude. My heart was so full after spending time in worship and prayer. I could physically *feel* Him close to me.

I went on to share my faith with unbelievers. When they asked me questions about the Bible, I would whisper in my heart, *Holy Spirit, give me the answer to their question so that You may be revealed to them.* I would begin to share whatever the Holy Spirit placed into my spirit, and their question would get answered. I remember thinking, *Where on earth did that come from?* The answers blew my mind, and I knew for a fact that they did not come from me.

As I grew in my relationship with the Holy Spirit, it became evident to others that something was different about me. Even my sixth-grade teacher was affected by the Spirit of God on my life. When my mum came to my parent-teacher interview to review my report card, she stopped my mother in the middle of their conversation and blurted out, "I have to say something about Alex. I have never seen this before on a child, but Alex has the light of God shining on her. I can see it when I look at her in the classroom. I cannot explain it, but she radiates the love of Jesus. Do you also see this on her?"

My mum smiled as she began to share about the person and

power of the Holy Spirit. My teacher was hungry to know more because she wanted this same light radiating through her. My mum was able to pray with her and for the power of the Holy Spirit to be on her life. It's amazing how the Holy Spirit enables us to be witnesses to those around us about the love and light of Jesus if we'll simply allow Him, with both our words and the way we live our lives.

When we are born again and filled with the Holy Spirit, it should be evident to others. Why is it, then, that so many Christians are afraid to share Jesus with the world? Why do we fail to let the power of almighty God be evidenced in and through us? As I look at the modern-day church, it's clear that many have either fallen asleep or taken a passive stance by choosing not to walk in the fullness of the Holy Spirit. We are meant to be carriers of the power of the Holy Spirit—the spirit of God who radiates from us and reveals a supernatural way of loving people that is vastly different from how the world operates. His Spirit transforms us personally and gives us a peace that surpasses all understanding—one that others can visibly notice.

We are meant to be carriers of the power of the Holy Spirit.

We must understand that it is not the wrath of God but rather His loving-kindness that brings people to repentance. It is His resurrection power that brings people into freedom, and it is the Holy Spirit who gives us boldness to share our faith. The Holy Spirit does the deep heart work of drawing that person to Himself. Our call is to simply step out in obedience.

I remember being around thirteen years old and one of my closest friends, Gabs, came to my house for a sleepover that we had been eagerly anticipating all week. In the middle of the night, she woke up having a horrible night terror, and I woke up to the sound of her crying. I went over to her and gently asked if I could pray over her. Gabs welcomed me to pray so I began to pray in tongues quietly as this had always helped me whenever I felt afraid in the nighttime. As I prayed, she told me she felt peace wash over her and that all fear immediately left as soon as I began to speak in this unknown language. When I stopped, she quickly asked me to keep praying because she was desperate for that feeling of peace to stay in the room. Even at that young age, I recognized the power the Holy Spirit had anointed me with—a power beyond my earthly understanding or comprehension. But I knew He was real. I knew He had power. And I knew I needed more of Him.

Others would confirm what was happening too. The Holy Spirit was real to me, and through that experience, Gabs could not deny that He was real. I learned early on that I could talk to the Holy Spirit as a best friend. As I would sit in prayer, wait, and listen for His prompting, He would guide me with a quiet whisper in my heart. He spoke to me through an inner voice. I have never heard Him audibly but I have sensed His voice speaking to the depths of my heart and spirit.

I could recognize when it was His voice and not my own because what He said was always wiser than my own thoughts. Then, when I would obey His instruction, it would result in something powerful and would often answer the very question I had been wrestling with. Little did I know just how much I was going to need the Divine Counselor throughout my life. As a young girl, I didn't fully understand the depth of that need yet.

I have written about my childhood and the many challenges

I had to overcome in my book *Tailor Made.* I was a sinner saved by grace, but I was still a prisoner to the strongholds in my mind. I went to church. I served as a faithful volunteer. I raised my hands and spoke in tongues, but the deep pain I carried influenced the most important parts of my life, and my self-esteem was being hijacked by the Enemy. He had me in a chokehold of lies that I believed about myself. Unfortunately, I didn't have the tools to help me at such a formative stage of my life.

As I matured in my understanding of the Holy Spirit's role and applied the truth of His Word in my life, I found healing. I learned over time what it means to be saved *and* set free. That is why I am writing this book. I want you to have the tools for transformation. I had to learn the hard way, but if you listen and apply the biblical principles outlined in this book, I promise you will live in peace and experience purpose in a way you never dreamed possible.

The Holy Spirit's role is to reveal truth, to bring conviction, to teach, and to guide us in every area of our lives. Ultimately, He longs for a relationship with us so He can lead us, comfort us, and strengthen us. Even though Scripture sometimes likens the Holy Spirit to fire, wind, or oil, He is not simply a substance. He is a person. He is God in Spirit form, who dwells within us. The intimacy and closeness He invites us into are for our benefit. As believers, we have access to Him in any and all circumstances—so we never have to feel alone. He is the best Counselor and the One who wants your freedom even more than you do.

The very core of who I am is found the more I get to know God Himself intimately and recognize His voice. As humans, the challenge is that we often find it difficult to relate to, or have a conversation with, an invisible God. I get it. Early on in my relationship with the Holy Spirit, it sometimes felt like I was speaking to an imaginary friend. But as I continued to lean in to this personal relationship, everything changed for me. I know it will be the same for you as well. As you develop this wonderful relationship over time, with consistent discipline, you will discover that you not only have a friend who sticks closer than a brother, but you also have the counsel of God at your disposal every day. As you develop your *friendship* with the Holy Spirit, He will radically change your life. He's calling you into this friendship. Are you willing to accept the invitation?

He is not simply a substance. He is a person.

THE DAY *THE* HOLY SPIRIT BECAME HOLY SPIRIT

My husband had grown up in church, but he never truly understood the personal relationship that was available with the Holy Spirit. He became a committed Christian just before his nineteenth birthday, and after a few years of being involved in our youth group, he was employed as the creative worship director. He had given his life to passionately serving the church and felt that he had developed a strong relationship with God.

In the winter of 1999, we had an unusually powerful youth camp. In fact, we kept the meetings going every night for six weeks after the camp weekend was over because God was moving in such powerful ways. Each night, the presence of God was tangible, thick in the room like a holy weight you could feel in your bones. Revival had broken out among our young adults.

Tears fell, chains broke, and lives were being transformed night after night. It feels impossible to adequately describe the radical life change we were witnessing.

One night, after one of those gatherings had ended, a friend came running over to Henry. He had experienced something that totally changed the way he personally related to God. When he was a young boy, his father walked out on their family. This loss created a void in his heart that made it difficult for him to relate to God intimately as a father. Despite believing in God, he struggled to experience his heavenly Father's love because his earthly father's love toward him had been so broken.

But this night, a revelation and spiritual transformation happened. He understood that God, through the Holy Spirit, could be everything his father hadn't been, and so much more. He told Henry that he felt the loving arms of God wrap around him like a Father who loves his son unconditionally and unequivocally. Years of abandonment issues and fears of rejection left his body. He finally understood what Jesus meant when He said He would send the Holy Spirit to be our Comforter, Advocate, and the One who would always be there for us. It was a profound moment for our friend that changed his life.

As Henry drove home later that night, after witnessing the breakthrough that just happened to his friend, he asked God why he'd never had experiences like that. He knew about God, but he longed to *know* God—profoundly, personally, and intimately. As soon as his lips uttered that prayer, he had the strangest sensation that someone else was in the car with him. He recalled that it felt like the same feeling you get when you're not facing the door, but know someone has just walked into the room. He glanced over to the passenger's seat, but no one was there. He fastened his eyes on the road again but still felt as if someone was physically in the car with him.

It wasn't long before he realized that God was helping him understand something more about Himself—something Henry had never understood before. Henry had always felt that "the Holy Spirit" was some mystical, out-there kind of force that did miraculous things in our lives but couldn't relate to him personally. As he sat there in his old white, beat-up panel van, the Holy Spirit began to converse with him in his heart. Through this inner voice, the Holy Spirit began to explain that He wasn't just a far-out-there, distant force. He was a person, and He wanted to be Henry's friend. The kind of friend he could turn to when everyone else let him down. The One who would be there to encourage him and spur him on when he needed it. The One who would be like Jesus walking alongside him, as if in the flesh.

Henry was puzzled at first and didn't know how to respond. So he said to the Holy Spirit, "I understand. You want to be my friend. But what do I say to You?"

He replied, *Ask Me how I am.*

"Ask You how You are?" Henry replied hesitantly.

Yes, He affirmed. *Ask Me how I am.*

So, he did. It felt as though a real person was sitting in the passenger seat, and they began to talk like two friends having a chat over a coffee, just hanging out together. He told Henry not to refer to Him as *the* Holy Spirit but to simply call Him *Holy Spirit* like it was His name—so Henry could begin to see Him as a person rather than some mysterious force. The entire drive home, they talked and talked like old friends who never got tired of each other.

As he approached our house, Holy Spirit asked him to do something that felt particularly strange. He asked him to walk up to the front door, knock, and wait for me to answer. When I answered the door, I saw Henry standing in front of me, smiling, with his arm wrapped tightly around an invisible person. Right there on our front porch, he began to introduce Holy Spirit to me. He told me that from now on, Holy Spirit was going to come and live in our home. He would be a part of our lives and the first person we would call on when we needed answers, guidance, or strength.

I will never forget how I felt in that moment. I could tangibly feel the presence of God. It was as if God Himself was standing before me, right next to my husband. I immediately began to weep as I stood in the doorway. After they came inside, we both walked down the hallway with our arms interlinked, our invisible God beside us. That night, we prayed and wept, acknowledging that whatever decision needed to be made, or whatever problem we would face, we would include Holy Spirit as our Counselor every time. I know this sounds crazy—and believe me, we felt crazy! But that night something changed in our household forever. Even now, twenty-six years later, one of the hallmarks of our home is that every person who walks through our doors says they sense the tangible presence of God.

Henry's life changed forever that night. His life and his relationship with God have been different ever since, because Henry finally understood what Jesus was talking about in the book of John. Holy Spirit is the Spirit of truth who will be a friend to you, just as Jesus was to His disciples here on earth. The best part is that He will never leave you nor forsake you!

> And I will ask the Father, and he will give you another advocate to help you and be with you forever—the Spirit of truth.

> The world cannot accept him, because it neither sees him nor knows him. But you know him, for he lives with you and will be in you. (John 14:16–17)

Holy Spirit wants to be your closest friend, your go-to confidant, and your Divine Counselor. As we move into the next chapter, you will see evidence in Scripture that proves He is a real person. This will help you demystify Him as a force and recognize Him as someone who is longing to have a relationship with you. As we continue this journey together, you will discover how He will guide you into all truth and give you the answers that you're so desperately seeking. Through His help, you will be able to navigate this life with supernatural wisdom and live in perfect harmony with God Himself.

Will you spend some time right now asking Him to reveal Himself to you so that you can begin this journey of having the Spirit of God with you every day of your life?

PRAYER

Holy Spirit, I am sorry that I never saw You as a person and found it hard to relate to You. I desire to know You this way and I am asking You to make Yourself known to me. I long to know You as a friend. Help me understand who You are and help me develop a relationship with You. I welcome You into every part of my life. Show me Your ways, and guide me in all truth, every day. In Jesus' name, amen.

CHAPTER 4

Holy Spirit Is Not a What, He's a Who

When learning about the person of Holy Spirit, we must first make sure we understand who He is according to Scripture and how we can relate to Him the same way we would to God the Father and Jesus Christ. He is not some mystical force to be afraid of or an ethereal presence you can't relate to. He is the Spirit of the living God, given to dwell within us. We cannot reduce Him to an object or describe Him incorrectly by avoiding personal pronouns. He is a person, and He has the power to liberate us, change us, lead us, and help us to look more like Jesus every day—if we learn His ways and obey His voice.

Jesus said it was better for Him to return to the Father so He could send us another Helper, Comforter, Counselor, and Guide—Holy Spirit (John 16:7). Yet as I've said before, I believe that in the church today, Holy Spirit is the most misunderstood and, sometimes, the most neglected within the Godhead. We serve a triune God: Father, Son, and Holy Spirit. Michael Reeves explained it like this:

> The Spirit's personal presence in us means we are brought to enjoy the Spirit's own intimate communion with the Father and the Son. If the Spirit were not God, He could not do that. It is all because God is three persons—Father, Son and Spirit—that we can have such communion. If God was in heaven and His Spirit a mere force, He would be more distant than the moon.[1]

Holy Spirit is fully personal, and because of this, we must be intentional about developing an intimate relationship with Him. How often do we find ourselves feeling alone, wishing we had a safe place to fall? Humanity's greatest longing is to belong. We all want to feel safe, seen, and secure, yet we tend to forget that the God of the universe, in Spirit, wants to commune with us. If God promised to never leave us nor forsake us, why do we often *feel* so lonely?

I'd like to propose to you that maybe it's because many of us don't truly understand the Person He is. And we don't understand the Person He is because we've either been taught that He's not active today, or that we should be fearful of Him. You might be thinking, *Why would anyone be afraid of Holy Spirit!?* As humans, we are often afraid of the unknown or what we cannot fully grasp with our minds. So instead of seeking Him for ourselves, we run and hide. We avoid Him. We think we're just fine doing this alone.

But when we do this, we neglect the one relationship that could be our very lifeline. We are rejecting the invitation to be radically transformed. We are saying no to knowing Him intimately as our best friend. If we only identify Him as wind, fire, or water, we fail to remember His personal attributes. He is one of three persons in the Godhead (Father, Son, and Holy Spirit), and Scripture confirms that He possesses the characteristics of a real person. And what makes a person a person? Let's take a look at what the Bible says.

HE HAS A MIND: HE KNOWS ALL THINGS

Holy Spirit is omniscient, which means He knows *everything*. He knows every detail about our lives—past, present, and future. One of the most profound ways we witness this is through the prophetic voice of God, which often comes through people. The Spirit of God moved through Jesus, who knew details about people and spoke words of knowledge that brought change to people's situations. His Spirit also revealed God's glory. Paul taught us about Holy Spirit, saying:

> These are the things God has revealed to us by his Spirit. The Spirit searches all things, even the deep things of God. For who knows a person's thoughts except their own spirit within them? In the same way no one knows the thoughts of God except the Spirit of God. What we have received is not the spirit of the world, but the Spirit who is from God, so that we may understand what God has freely given us. This is what we speak, not in words taught us by human wisdom but in words taught by the Spirit, explaining spiritual realities with Spirit-taught words. (1 Corinthians 2:10–14)

In John 4, Jesus came across a Samaritan woman at a well. There's something truly powerful about this story because Jesus was a Jew, and Jewish people did not associate with Samaritans.

At that time in history, a Jewish man, especially a rabbi, would never converse with a woman like this. Yet Jesus found Himself being led to this particular well in the middle of the day and asked her for a drink.

At first, she was stunned. I imagine all the thoughts that must've been swirling around in her head: *Wait, did He just talk to me? First, He's a Jew. Second, He's a rabbi. Third, why is He even here right now? It's the hottest time of the day. No one ever comes here during this time. Now this guy is approaching me and wants to get to know me . . . What is going on here?*

When Jesus asked her to give Him a drink, she replied, "You are a Jew and I am a Samaritan woman. How can you ask *me* for a drink?" (v. 9, emphasis mine). She also added, "You have nothing to draw with and the well is deep" (v. 11).

According to tradition, a Jew would never touch anything previously touched by a Samaritan because it would have been deemed unclean. Yet here, Jesus broke all cultural norms. He began a conversation with this woman so He could introduce Himself as her God—her personal God. He went on to share that the water He had for her was living water, and that if she drank it, she'd never thirst again.

Upon hearing Jesus' words, the woman assumed that having this living water meant she'd never have to return to the well and draw water again. Yet she still didn't realize who she was speaking with. Jesus then asked her to go call her husband and return to the well. She replied, "I have no husband." Jesus said to her, "You are right when you say you have no husband. The fact is, you have had five husbands, and the man you now have is not your husband. What you have just said is quite true." The woman replied, "I can see that you are a prophet" (vv. 17–19).

How did Jesus know this about the woman? How was He able to speak truths about her that she never told Him? How was this stranger able to read her mail—all of it? Even though they'd never met, it was the Spirit *in* Jesus who knew every detail of her life. The Spirit of God is omniscient; therefore, He knows all things—even the things that we may be afraid to admit to the people around us, or the issues we're afraid to confront within ourselves. But what I love about Jesus is that He did not reveal this information to expose or shame her. Rather, He wanted to reveal Himself to her and heal her heart. For years, she bounced from relationship to relationship, desperately trying to fill the void in her heart. Men had rejected her. Society had disgraced her. She'd been searching for love, hope, and purpose in all the wrong places. But now, the Creator of her purpose was standing in front of her, offering her a new way. A better way. *The* way.

Jesus, led by the Spirit, introduced Himself to her so He could save her soul, redeem her life, and heal her longing for true love. After that supernatural interaction, she went back to her town and shared her testimony, which caused many to believe in Jesus Christ.

She told the Samaritans what Jesus said to her and how He told her everything she had ever done. Because of her testimony, many believed! Jesus went on to stay two more days in that place. After the other Samaritans personally encountered Jesus, they exclaimed, "We no longer believe just because of what you said; now we have heard for ourselves, and we know that this man really is the Savior of the world" (John 4:42). Holy Spirit knows everything, and when we tap into His Spirit, He searches all things and reveals the truth. This often brings conviction to hearts, which leads to salvation. When people become saved through the work of Christ on the cross, God is glorified, and people find freedom in Jesus.

I have personally experienced the omniscient power of God and His Spirit, who works through believers and knows all things. There have been countless times when someone has prayed with me and spoken things over me that no one else could have known except God. I've received messages from the Lord through people that were personal, direct, and supernatural. God often uses His Spirit, working in and through people, to deliver a word of encouragement, confirmation, or edification straight from heaven. This is one of the many reasons I'm so thankful to serve a God who is both personal and relational.

I've also been on the other side. For as long as I can remember, God has been revealing things to me in my spirit for others. As I would pray for a certain person, the Lord would impress upon my heart specific things that made no sense to me. Yet, I could sense the Spirit was telling me these things to encourage them or to reveal God to them. Holy Spirit wants to encourage people by speaking to them through men and women of faith. He also longs to reveal mysteries to us personally through the Word of God. Holy Spirit has the mind of God. Therefore, He wants us to live tethered to the mind of Christ so we can be continually transformed into His likeness (2 Corinthians 3:17–18).

HE HAS EMOTIONS: HE CAN BE GRIEVED

> And do not grieve the Holy Spirit of God, with whom you were sealed for the day of redemption. Get rid of all bitterness, rage and anger, brawling and slander, along with every form

> of malice. Be kind and compassionate to one another, forgiving each other, just as in Christ God forgave you. (Ephesians 4:30–32)

There was a season in my young adult life when I had one foot in the world (flesh) and one foot in the kingdom (spirit). When your flesh is not fully surrendered, it will always be at war with your spirit. I remember living like this for several years. I loved God, but I still wanted to do things my way.

I had just finished high school, and I was trying to figure out who I was in the transition of becoming a young adult. I was living with a divided heart, and for four years, I experienced constant inner turmoil. I felt like I was on an emotional roller coaster. I made decisions that brought harm and chaos to my life. I pretended to be enjoying my supposed "freedom," doing whatever I pleased, yet suffering the inevitable consequences. I was lying to my parents and living a double life. I would go to clubs and bars with friends Saturday night and walk into church Sunday morning feeling the guilt of the decisions I had made the night before.

I felt confused about who I was and what I was supposed to do with my life. The only way I knew to escape the fears and questions tormenting my mind was to run from them. I felt anxious all the time and had no direction or sense of purpose. I was wandering aimlessly, hoping it would all just fall into place.

After graduating from high school, I attended a legal secretarial college. Rather than boldly living out my faith, I hid it and blended in with the crowd. I was broken and desperately trying to find meaning in life. Was I a church attendee with one foot in the world, enjoying life on my terms? Or was I a devout follower of Jesus, living a life of complete surrender to Him? I was torn between these two paradigms. It wasn't until one night that I encountered Jesus in a nightclub and He brought me to a point of decision. In the midst of flashing lights, smoke dancing in the air, and "Ride on Time" by Black Box booming through the speakers, Holy Spirit, in a gentle and loving whisper, spoke directly to my heart.[2] *Alex,* He said, *What are you doing here?* I froze. *This is not who I called you to be*, He said.

I knew at that moment that I was grieving Holy Spirit by being at that club, surrounded by people bound in their sin and brokenness. There was immorality everywhere I turned. Even though I had been running away from Him in this season of my life, the Spirit within me was still sensitive to His voice. When He spoke clearly to me in the middle of that club, my perspective completely changed.

I began to see everything and everyone around me differently. Where I previously saw men and women dancing just to unwind and have fun, I now saw what looked like zombies aimlessly and desperately trying to feel something. They were alive on the outside but dead on the inside. I began to clearly see the brokenness all around me. My heart broke for these people, and I knew *I* was breaking God's heart by being there. His voice arrested me so intently that I grabbed my purse, left my boyfriend and friends without even telling them, and drove straight home. I made a decision that night: I couldn't keep living like this.

When I got to my room, I took my finger, drew a line in the pink plush carpet on my floor, and literally stepped over it as a sign to God that I was never going back. I confessed my double-minded living and surrendered my entire heart to

Him. As I sat there on my bedroom floor, I heard God say to me, *Alex, you have given Me a part of your heart, but not all of your heart. In order for Me to give you the life you are dreaming about—a life of freedom and wholeness—you must leave behind the worldly patterns and follow My lead.* This was an invitation, not a demand, and I had a choice to make. Was I going to stay in the place I was in, or live as a true disciple of Jesus, wholeheartedly serving Him?

That night at twenty years of age, I gave my *whole* heart to Jesus, no longer living divided with one foot in the world and the other in church. I decided to make Jesus my Lord, which meant I would listen and obey everything He asked me to do. If He has lordship in our lives, that means we can't be the lord over our own lives. He's either the God of everything or He's the God of nothing in our lives. The key to true freedom is making Him *both Savior and Lord.*

> The key to true freedom is making Him *both Savior and Lord.*

The first thing He asked me to do was break up with my boyfriend at the time, who would not propel me into the future God had for me. Then, He asked me to leave those friends behind. Please hear me, friend. People can be good *to* you, but not good *for* you. The company you keep matters. Psalm 1:1–2 says, "Blessed is the one who does not walk in step with the wicked or stand in the way that sinners take or sit in the company of mockers, but whose delight is in the law of the Lord, and who meditates on his law day and night."

As a believer, if the people around you don't challenge and encourage you to be more in love with Jesus, then it's time for some new friends. I know this is hard and takes courage, but you're not alone. Holy Spirit will help you and empower you to do what you can't do on your own. He desires to bring godly friends and community into your life. Ask Him for the right connections.

Last, God asked me to get alone with Him and deal with the root issues of my pain. I had been partying to cover up a void in my heart, and Jesus wanted to heal me. When I finally came to the point of surrender, I experienced hope and healing beyond anything I had dreamed possible. I have never looked back, and my life is beyond anything I could have imagined—simply because I followed His lead. It hasn't been easy. It has taken time, consistency, and commitment, and a determination not to give up. Holy Spirit has taught me how to walk out my salvation with Him. The process was costly, but it has been beyond rewarding. Much like the disciples, we all have a choice. We can either leave everything behind to follow this man named Jesus or we can choose to remain stuck, aimlessly searching in vain for what we all long for: peace and purpose.

What does it mean to grieve the Holy Spirit? To grieve someone simply means hurting their feelings or causing sorrow by our actions. When we act in a way that opposes the nature of God and is outside of His will, we hurt God's heart—because we're not reflecting who He is to the world. If we are born again, with Christ living within us, then we have the choice to reflect more of Him and less of our former self-serving flesh.

When we accept Christ, the Bible says we put off our "old self" and put on "the new self," which is created to be like God in true righteousness and holiness (Ephesians 4:22–24). However, when we choose to live in immorality, disobedience, anger, or dishonesty, we cause the Lord grief. Our actions break God's heart because He knows He created us for more, and our decisions bring burdens instead of blessings.

Paul described the type of behavior that grieves Holy Spirit. He urged the church in Ephesus not to think or live according to the world. The people had lost all sensitivity by hardening their hearts and giving themselves over to sexual immorality. They were operating in the flesh rather than the Spirit. With love and correction, Paul instructed them to put off their old self and put on their new self, which thinks and acts in holiness the way God designed.

If you have grieved the Holy Spirit or are currently grieving the Holy Spirit, and feel convicted even now, be quick to repent and ask for forgiveness. Ask Him to help you live according to God's way and not your own. He is your Helper. As the Divine Counselor, He will teach you how to live according to the Spirit rather than your flesh. He will give you the grace to live righteously when you ask Him and obey His still, small voice.

HE HAS A WILL: HE CONVICTS THE WORLD OF SIN

> But very truly I tell you, it is for your good that I am going away. Unless I go away, the Advocate will not come to you; but if I go, I will send him to you. When he comes, he will prove the world to be in the wrong about sin and righteousness and judgment: about sin, because people do not believe in me; about righteousness, because I am going to the Father, where you can see me no longer; and about judgment, because the prince of this world now stands condemned. (John 16:7–11)

The Divine Counselor is always drawing us to become more like Jesus, and in doing so, He speaks to our inner man. We all have a conscience, whether we are believers or not. Our conscience is our inner moral compass that helps us navigate right from wrong. Conviction from the Holy Spirit, however, is His direct and powerful work within us to expose sin and lead us to repentance. The Holy Spirit convicts us not to condemn us but to bring awareness of our own sin and the error of our ways. His desire and will are always to make us more Christlike. He wants to be the internal compass that leads and guides us into all truth (our true north) that will help us make decisions that will bear good fruit in our lives.

Conviction often manifests as a sense of unease or at the realization that our actions are wrong and not pleasing to God. It should stir in us a desire to change for the better. It often comes through an impression on our heart, and we have a choice to respond to it or not. If we continue to ignore these impressions, we can move toward developing a seared conscience—a conscience that has become hardened or insensitive to guilt or remorse, often due to repeated wrongdoing. It's like a conscience that has been cauterized and no longer feels the internal check in our heart when we do something wrong. This desensitization can be a result of ignoring or rejecting the inner voice that prompts us to recognize our actions as wrong or right. This is a dangerous place to live, and we must make sure our inner man stays sensitive to the voice of Holy Spirit.

When the Spirit of God lives in us, He convicts us when we do something that is not in His nature—gossip or slander, for example. Have you ever found yourself speaking ill of someone and immediately felt a check in your heart? You feel convicted because if God were physically standing in the middle of your conversation, you would probably refrain from saying those things. Or if that person were standing right in front of you, you would think twice about what comes out of your mouth.

Here's another example. If the Holy Spirit were in your bedroom while you were watching something you shouldn't be watching, would you still watch it if He were physically in the room? Probably not. We must live constantly aware of the presence of God in our lives so we are more sensitive to His conviction and can quickly change course.

Conviction is different from condemnation, and we should be careful not to confuse the two. Conviction is a feeling of guilt or wrongdoing that leads to repentance and change. Condemnation, on the other hand, produces a sense of personal worthlessness and hopelessness. It makes us feel judged and void of any grace and mercy, which in turn hinders growth and repentance. Condemnation often comes from the Enemy's voice; whereas conviction comes from the voice of Holy Spirit.

Now that we have established that Holy Spirit is in fact the third person of the Godhead, I want to show you how He helps us develop an intimate relationship with Him.

HOLY SPIRIT REVEALS JESUS

One of the ways Holy Spirit helps us is by revealing Jesus. Scripture teaches that it is Holy Spirit who illuminates our hearts so we can see Jesus for who He really is. Holy Spirit doesn't want to be worshiped. He wants to help you worship Jesus. Holy Spirit wants us to know Jesus and helps us remember His words so they can transform us. The more you develop a relationship with Holy Spirit, the more in love with Jesus you become. This love is manifested as a desire to know Him more deeply and, in turn, reflect who He is to the world around you.

Holy Spirit ensures that the spotlight is always on Jesus. He teaches us how to bear fruit that reveals Christ through our lives. As we grow in intimacy with Him, Jesus becomes more real to us than ever before. This is all made possible because of Holy Spirit's work within us. Any person or church who places a greater emphasis on Holy Spirit than Jesus has created an imbalanced theology. Holy Spirit has always been there to point us back to Jesus, who holds the resurrection power that sets us free.

Holy Spirit doesn't want to be worshiped. He wants to help you worship Jesus.

HE SPEAKS AND TEACHES US

> But when he, the Spirit of truth, comes, he will guide you into all the truth. He will not speak on his own; he will speak only what he hears, and he will tell you what is yet to come. (John 16:13)

When Holy Spirit speaks to us, it will never contradict the Word of God. All Scripture is God-breathed, which means Holy Spirit only speaks what the Word of God says. He cannot speak apart from God the Father and the Son. Therefore, He always speaks the truth. I often hear people repeat the lie about themselves that they are insignificant or that their life doesn't matter.

You will not find one verse in Scripture that validates this. Yet the Enemy often comes and whispers lies into our minds, trying to convince us that we have no value in this world. This is absolutely contrary to what the Word of God says about us.

> So God created man in his own image,
> in the image of God he created them;
> male and female he created them. (Genesis 1:27)

This verse establishes that humans are created in God's image, reflecting a special relationship and inherent value within each individual person. Regardless of how you feel or the words that have been spoken over you, *this* is the truth regarding who you really are. So, the next time you hear something negative that condemns or makes you feel insignificant, ask Holy Spirit to speak and reveal the truth of His Word to you.

> All Scripture is God-breathed and is useful for teaching, rebuking, correcting and training in righteousness, so that the servant of God may be thoroughly equipped for every good work. (2 Timothy 3:16–17)

The Bible is a supernatural work of God. Think about this: The sixty-six books of the Bible were written by forty authors from diverse backgrounds, living over a period of about fifteen hundred years, and yet when all sixty-six books are brought together, they form one complete, unified story from beginning to end. This shows me that the God of the universe, by the Spirit of God, supernaturally breathed each page into existence through the men who wrote each and every word. When Holy

Spirit illuminates the Scriptures to us, He is speaking just as He spoke to the men who wrote the Scriptures under the inspiration of the Spirit of God.

> Open my eyes, that I may behold
> wondrous things out of your law.
> (Psalm 119:18 ESV)

When we read Scripture, we need Holy Spirit to shine a light on both the mysteries and the revelation of Jesus. *Revelation* simply means the unveiling of something hidden that is meant to be discovered. Holy Spirit acts as a light that illuminates the darkness of our spiritual understanding, making God's Word clear and understandable.

I remember my Bible college professor teaching us to pray before we ever opened the Bible. I would pray, *Holy Spirit, open my eyes to Your Word and make it come alive in me.* As the Holy Spirit shines a light on God's Word, He brings revelation, which ultimately leads to the transformation of our lives. This is why it is imperative to read and study the Word of God ourselves so then we will know when Holy Spirit is speaking to us. Anything contrary to the Word of God should not resonate with our spirit. I expound more on how to hear the voice of God in chapter 9.

HE ADVOCATES

> But the Advocate, the Holy Spirit, whom the Father will send in my name, will teach you all things and will remind you of everything I have said to you. (John 14:26)

In the legal profession, *advocate* refers to a lawyer who actively represents a client in court, presenting their case by arguing on their behalf, examining witnesses, and ensuring their legal rights are protected throughout the process. Essentially, they speak for the client and work to achieve the best possible outcome based on the law and available evidence. Just as we might ask a human lawyer for legal advice before doing something, we should ask the Holy Spirit to be our legal counselor as we live our lives.

The spiritual world is set up much like a legal system. The Enemy accuses us before the Judge—who is God—and Holy Spirit steps in to defend us against the accusations. The blood of Jesus is like evidence in the courtroom of heaven that speaks on your behalf. Regardless of what you've done, Jesus paid the price so you wouldn't have to—so you could be seen as righteous in the Father's eyes. Holy Spirit is your advocate and speaks for you when you can't speak for yourself.

HE INTERCEDES FOR US

> **All my longings lie open before you, Lord;**
> **my sighing is not hidden from you.**
> **(Psalm 38:9)**

When we don't know how to pray—when all we can offer is a sigh, groan, or the feeling of being at the end of our rope—that is when Holy Spirit steps in and becomes like our breath when it feels like we can't breathe. There have been times when I've been so overwhelmed by grief and anxious thoughts I couldn't find words to pray, so I began to pray in the Spirit (in my heavenly language). It felt as if He took over and interceded alongside me. We have Holy Spirit, who helps us breathe, groaning and aching on our behalf, presenting our requests before God in heaven. He is already in the future, interceding for us, calling those things which are not as though they were. Paul wrote, "In the same way, the Spirit helps us in our weakness. We do not know what we ought to pray for, but the Spirit himself intercedes for us through wordless groans" (Romans 8:26).

Have you ever felt such a heavy burden for someone you love that you didn't know what else to do except bring them before the Lord in prayer? In the Bible, *intercession* refers to the act of praying or pleading on behalf of others. Essentially, when you intercede for someone, you act as a mediator or advocate between God and them, seeking His mercy and intervention on their behalf. Knowing that Holy Spirit stands in the gap for us when we don't have the strength to pray is so comforting to me. Jesus, who sits at the right hand of the Father, is also interceding for us. As believers, we are called to intercede in prayer for those around us.

I hope that as we conclude this chapter, our journey through Scripture together has given you both a theological understanding and a personal revelation of who Holy Spirit really is. I've said it before, but it bears repeating. He's not a mystical force. He is a person, and He wants to walk this journey of life with you—if you'll let Him.

Maybe this chapter was a lot to process, and perhaps you're getting to know Holy Spirit in a new light. Or maybe you've always related to Him as a person. Either way, I believe He wants to reveal Himself to you in even deeper ways.

Before we learn more about our Divine Counselor, would

you take a few moments, close your eyes, and invite Holy Spirit to continue this journey with you? It may feel a little strange at first, but I know that His heart is to become your close friend. He longs to have an intimate relationship with you. All it takes is turning your affection toward Him, just as you would toward someone who means the world to you. Wait for Him to respond—either by an impression in your heart or a picture in your mind. When you open up the Scriptures, ask Holy Spirit to illuminate words that speak life into your very being. Let's pray.

PRAYER

Holy Spirit, thank You for being my Advocate, Helper, Counselor, and Friend. I believe that You will guide me into all truth, so I ask as I continue reading Your Word, navigate life's challenges, and grow in my faith, that You would lead me every step of the way. Forgive me for the times I haven't seen You for who You truly are. I repent for the moments when I've grieved You. Thank You for Your mercy and grace. Holy Spirit, help me see Jesus clearly and grant me understanding of Your Word. I honor You, and I invite You to join me on this journey of sanctification. In Jesus' name, amen.

CHAPTER 5

The Mother Heart of Father God

Can we be honest? Have you ever felt so abandoned, disappointed, or overwhelmed by a situation that you blamed God? Maybe you cried out for help, but the heavens felt like brass. You wondered if every prayer just bounced back off a hard, heavenly surface and slipped away into the abyss. Nothing seemed to work, and the more you cried out, the more twisted in knots you became. You felt like a child who had been abandoned, and all you longed for was a soft place to land—loving arms that would bring comfort to the war going on inside you.

I get it. I've been there too. For several years, I walked through a dark season where I was in a desperate and lonely place, with no hope of escape from this pit. I felt like I had no one to talk to, so my default was to blame God for my loneliness. I had buried myself in a cave of isolation that felt like a prison. I had been believing for a breakthrough in the life of a family member I'd been praying for over the course of seven years. The situation felt so out of control that I consistently found myself wanting to manipulate it, but I was in over my head.

The more I prayed for this situation to change, the worse it seemed to get. I was in survival mode, struggling to trust God in the midst of it all. I became anxious and lost sleep, tossing and turning every night. I was paralyzed with fear, overcome by worry, and unable to shake the feeling of dread. I tried to reason and argue my perspective, trying to convince this person that they were on the wrong path. But the more I intervened, the worse the situation became. I hit a breaking point. I was weary, exhausted, and felt like giving up on life. The words swirling around in my head sounded like, *It would be better if you just left this earth. Your heart can't take another blow. Just end it, and you won't have to wake up to this ache in your heart anymore.*

My heart was beating at a speed I knew was unhealthy. I was still functioning in my work life, but my soul felt like it had been torn to pieces and stomped on until there was nothing left of me. During that season, I got a call from my mum after she watched me preach via livestream one Sunday. She said, "Alex, you are wearing a spirit of heaviness. I can see it all over you, and I know that you are not doing well." To the average person watching me, I seemed fine. I was preaching, traveling, and ministering out of my weakness. But my mum, through the Spirit's leading, could tell something was wrong.

God's grace was so evident in that season, and He carried me through some of my darkest days. When all I wanted to do was go to sleep and hope I never woke up, He was still there. Yes, there were days when I wished God would take me home so I didn't have to feel the pain anymore. I felt like I was suffocating. The fear and dread consumed my soul. I was not thinking straight regarding this issue. Words came out of my mouth that were ugly and hurtful, but I didn't know what else to do. My husband would allow me to process with him, but when my words became curses, he would gently stop me and say, "Please stop cursing the situation."

I responded, "I just can't help it. I am so hurt and so angry. It feels like God is not answering my prayers." I found myself constantly saying things like, "I am done." "I give up." "This is not fair." "I have given everything to God, and this is what I get in return." "It's not worth it." "I hate this so much." Even though I was praying, my prayers were not effective. Why weren't they working? Why was I seemingly getting worse while the situation remained unchanged?

After finding out some alarming details one night, I thought that might be what would push me over the edge. I remember lying on my bathroom floor, weeping uncontrollably. I can honestly say that at this point I did not want to be alive anymore. I could not see the light at the end of this very long, dark tunnel. All I could see was what was in front of me: a dark and horrible problem that felt like it would never go away. I sank onto the cold tiles on the floor, threw my fist up at God, and accused Him, saying, "You are unfaithful. You made me a promise that if I took care of our church, You would take care of my family. You have failed on Your end of the bargain, and I am angry with You."

As soon as I uttered those words, I knew that I had grieved Holy Spirit. Even though it felt like a release in the moment, I felt sick as soon as the words left my mouth. Deep down, I knew what my lips had just uttered was a lie. But this is often what happens when our souls are so burdened with pain that we go to our default—whatever that may be. For many of us, our sinful nature rises up because we've allowed our flesh to dictate how we feel rather than allowing the Spirit of God to lead us in the actual truth of the moment.

As I was weeping and feeling worse than ever before, I heard a still, small voice that echoed into the very chambers of my heart. *Alex,* He whispered, *You can't say that I am unfaithful. And the reason you can't say this is because I am not finished yet. You can't call Me unfaithful until it is over, and the story is not finished.*

As soon as I heard this in my heart, I cried even harder. I realized that Holy Spirit was speaking truth to my heart and mind. Even though the situation did not turn around in that moment, I felt the comfort and ministry of His love. I also realized that I had tried to make a deal with God, and in doing so, I had set myself up with an expectation I felt He was not meeting.

I believe many of us do this. We put timelines on God and expect Him to meet the deadline on our terms. We make deals with God that He never agreed to in the first place. Then, when things don't work out as we want them to, we blame God. We think He is unfaithful and unjust, but that is incorrect theology. We can't lower the nature of God to our human experience. My Bible says, "He is the Rock, his works are perfect, and all his ways are just. A faithful God who does no wrong, upright and just is he" (Deuteronomy 32:4).

God is never wrong. His ways are not our ways, and His thoughts are not our thoughts. A situation may be bad, but that doesn't mean God's character is bad. There are going to be seasons we walk through that are not good, but God's character is always good. It is who He is. He cannot be anything else. His faithfulness is tied to His goodness, even if the circumstances in our lives try to dictate otherwise.

When I was in this pit of despair, engaging with the Enemy and believing his lies that God was not being faithful to me and my family, I had to stop and allow Holy Spirit to correct my thinking. There was a war raging in my thought life. You may feel anger deep in your soul like I did and that is okay. Anger is an emotion that needs to be processed with the Lord. Sometimes, when we are full of anger, it is difficult to feel or hear from Holy Spirit, but when we bring our anger to Him, He can handle it. And when we do, He helps us get to the root of it, like He did with me. Once I finally stopped listening to the Enemy and leaned into Holy Spirit's voice, I had to make a decision. Would I believe *His* Word instead of *my* thoughts? I remember feeling a nudge from Holy Spirit telling me to call my friend and mentor, Debbie, who lived in Australia. She always gave me wise counsel, and I trusted the fruit of her life. She had overcome similar situations to what I was facing at the time, so I knew this directive was from the Lord.

His faithfulness is tied to His goodness, even if the circumstances in our lives try to dictate otherwise.

During times of chaos and confusion, it is critically important to choose your counsel wisely—those who will speak into our lives. Do not choose people who only tell you what you want to hear and affirm your wrong thinking. Instead, go to someone who isn't afraid to call you out and speak the truth in love. Humble yourself enough to realize that sometimes you need correcting, and the best thing you can do is listen with an open heart. Besides, let's face it. Nothing else was working for me at this point in my life. So I called Debbie and explained the horror of the situation.

She listened while I rambled, cried, and poured out all my feelings. She gracefully waited until I was done speaking, and all I heard on the other end was silence for a few seconds. Her pause felt like an eternity. Then she said two things that were incredibly profound. First, she said, "Alex, I'm sorry. But what I am hearing is that you are praying into this situation from a place of fear, not faith. When you pray from fear, you open the realm of the demonic to wreak havoc over your mind and the situation. The currency of heaven is faith. When we don't have faith, we cannot please God with the words that are coming out of our mouths."

Second, she said, "You are in the way of this situation, and you are controlling the narrative because of your fear. If you do not relinquish control and allow this person to fail, you will never give them the opportunity to exercise self-control, which is a fruit of the Spirit."

It was like a light switch had turned on in the dark night of my soul. She was right! In fact, she was so right that I just wept over the phone because I knew this was the word of the Lord. Even though I did not want to hear it, I knew it was what I needed. Debbie then added, "Let's pray." She began to pray with power and authority, like only she could. As she interceded and stepped into the gap left by my lack of faith, I simply received and agreed with every word that came out of her mouth. The Comforter, Holy Spirit, was ministering to my soul and spirit in that moment, and the flood of tears washed over me like fresh living water.

As we finished the conversation, she said to me, "You know what to do. Go into your prayer closet, shift your prayers from fear, and pray from a place of faith. If fear is your filter, you will not hear God correctly. Watch as God begins His work in you first—doing more within you than in the person you're hoping to see change." After we prayed, I hung up the phone. I wept some more and I played a worship song titled "Take It to Jesus."[1] I had the song on repeat as I let the Comforter and the Nurturer heal the wounded places of fear.

I allowed Him to fill my heart with perfect love before I prayed. I got up from my bedroom floor, wiped the tears from my eyes, and began to pray. But this time it was different. I prayed with faith and declared the promises of God over this person until I felt a shift in my spirit. I also prayed over myself—that I would no longer control or manipulate, but instead surrender and release the situation into the hands of the One who holds everything together and makes everything good in His time.

A few months later, the Lord led me to open my Bible to Joshua 11. When I got to the end of the chapter, I read words that felt like the audible voice of God through the illumination of Holy Spirit: "So Joshua took the entire land, just as the LORD directed Moses, and he gave it as an inheritance to Israel according to the tribal divisions. *Then the land had rest from war*" (v. 23, emphasis mine). When I read that last line, I wept deeply as I felt the soothing words of Holy Spirit say to my heart, *You have been in spiritual warfare for seven years, and now, because you have released control and prayed from a posture of faith, you can finally rest in Me. Watch what I can do when you choose to rest in My will and take the posture of faith by fully trusting Me with your family.* Within five months, I saw the situation I had been praying about for over seven years change. God changed my heart first, and then He changed this person's life in the most miraculous and unexpected way.

God is faithful to complete what He starts. I just needed to get out of the way and change the posture of my prayers. That summer, a few months after the miracle had manifested, I traveled through Europe with my family. I had always wanted to visit the Swiss Alps and summit a mountain, and that we did. It was the most breathtaking view I had ever experienced. As a small person—just five foot six inches—on top of a mountain ten thousand feet above ground level, surrounded by the summits of the Alps in that region, my immediate reaction was to cry.

I could hardly breathe because I was so overcome by the beauty and grandeur of God's creation. I felt the presence of God in the most profound way. I imagine this is what Moses, Abraham, David, and Elijah must have felt like when they met God on the mountain. I closed my eyes and, with tears streaming down my face, I repented before the Lord as I stood on a mountain that He created by speaking it into being—a mountain so grand and spectacular that it made me feel small and childlike.

Being there shifted my perspective and reminded me that God is so much bigger than anything I will ever face. If He spoke this mountain into being with His words, then He can do anything. How could I have ever doubted Him? I was heartbroken that I had made my problems seem bigger than Him. I am not exaggerating when I tell you that, in that very moment, my life changed. My faith went from being tossed by the wind to concrete and fully convinced. I had faith in the past, but it had limitations because of the lies that I had believed about God's nature. That is the most dangerous place we can be as believers—when we lower our theology to fit our experience. God is either who He says He is, or He is not. His blood either has the power to destroy the devil's work or it doesn't. He is the One who can heal our depression, anxiety, bipolar disorder, dysfunction, and broken heart or He isn't. It is on us to shift our perspective, and my friend, that only happens when we choose to surrender. It's only then that we allow Holy Spirit to reveal just how great our God is compared to our circumstances.

As I stood on the top of that mountain, it felt like God came down and comforted me as a mother comforts her child. I felt safe. I felt seen. I felt heard. I felt as if He had wrapped His arms around me like a mother does a child who comes home from school after being bullied.

I believe we all long to have a mother whose lap we can collapse into and whose arms we can sob in without judgment. We all need a safe person who receives us full of mercy and grace. When we are not rooted and established in God's nurturing love—this deep and sacred love—we will always be searching for it. We will never be satisfied with anything else. We will continually be on a quest for it, looking in all the wrong places. Our romantic relationships may give us a certain degree of fulfillment, but there will always be a deeper need gnawing at our soul. To see true transformation and healing in our lives, we must be willing to be nurtured by Holy Spirit and this requires us to understand that God carries the nurturing heart of a mother inside Him. Let me introduce you to the mother heart of Father God.

WE ARE MADE IN HIS IMAGE

> Then God said, "Let us make mankind in our image, in our likeness, so that they may rule." . . . So God created mankind in his own image, in the image of God he created them; male and female he created them. (Genesis 1:26–28)

If we are made in the image of God as this passage says, then God's nature carries both male and female attributes. God embodies the fullness of both—the femininity of God, as well as the masculinity of God. Sometimes, we do not receive the fullness of God's love because we see Him only through the lens of our father, but not our *mother.* A healthy mother and father raise children who are secure. This was God's original design for the family and the way God formed us gives us revelation of what His character is like.

Our need as humans is not only for a father but also for a mother. A male and a female, together, reflect the complete, full nature of God. If you've had a negative experience with your parents, you may need to disregard everything you've ever thought about your mother and father in order to see God for who He truly is. If you are a single parent reading this, the Lord has grace for you. He is "a father to the fatherless, a defender of widows, is God in his holy dwelling. God sets the lonely in families" (Psalm 68:5–6). No matter your family circumstance, I invite you to come to the Lord through Holy Spirit with a clean slate, because if not, you'll miss the true nature of our God—both masculine and feminine.

The use of feminine metaphors for the Holy Spirit has roots in biblical language and traditions. The Hebrew word for "spirit," *ruach*, is feminine, and this has influenced some interpretations of the Holy Spirit in early Christian and Jewish traditions.[2] Some see this as a representation of the Holy Spirit's nurturing, compassionate, and creative aspects, mirroring feminine attributes. It is worth saying from the outset, in the words of Jesus, "God is spirit" (John 4:24).[3]

John Piper said about this profound truth: "God is not male. . . . I mean that from eternity, God has not had a body—a physical body—and, therefore, he doesn't have male features: facial hair, musculature, . . . no Y chromosome, no male hormones, things like that. 'Male' is a biological word, and God is not a biological being."[4]

God the Father is Spirit. He created man and woman in His own image, though He Himself is neither male nor female. His heart is reflected in both the masculine and the feminine. He prefers to manifest His nature to us through masculine titles, and sometimes through feminine metaphors. For example, in the Bible, particularly in the book of Proverbs, wisdom is often personified as a woman and referred to with feminine pronouns. This is primarily due to the Hebrew word for "wisdom," *hokhmah*, which is grammatically feminine.[5] When King Solomon personified wisdom, he used feminine pronouns to align with the grammatical gender of the Hebrew word, creating a vivid image and emphasizing the blessings of being wise.

In C. S. Lewis's book *The Four Loves*, he explained the four expressions of love. We know *agape* (unconditional), *phileo* (friendship), and *eros* (romantic love). Then there is *storge* love (empathy/bond / familial love). This fourth love refers to strong and natural instinctive affection, like a mother's love nurturing an infant. It is the love that lays a healthy foundation for growth and maturity. Storge love speaks of nurture, compassion, gentleness, affection, and tenderness. C. S. Lewis said, "Storge love is the most organic and has the most comfortable and least ecstatic of the loves. It is to our emotions as a pair of slippers or like putting our worn track pants at home on or sinking into a comfortable sofa is to our bodies."[6]

Even though this Greek word *storge* is not specifically written in the Scriptures, the concept is found there many times, depicting familial love for one another. *Storge* love awakens the feminine heart of God in each of us. It calls a child into nurture, acceptance, belonging, and life. A mother who is healthy and whole teaches her children how to both love and be loved. If we did not receive sufficient *storge* love as a child, we find it difficult to be intimate with God and others.

If you're still unsure about the mother heart of Father God, I want to show you precedent in Scripture. Look at how the following verses reveal the nurturing and comforting attributes of God. God desires that we run to Him for comfort and rest in His love.

> "Come to me, all you who are weary and burdened, and I will give you rest. For my yoke is easy, and my burden is light." (Matthew 11:28–30)

> "How often I wanted to gather your children together, the way a hen gathers her chicks under her wings, and you were unwilling." (Matthew 23:37 NASB)

> But Zion said, "The LORD has forsaken me,
> the LORD has forgotten me.
> Can a mother forget the baby at her breast
> and have no compassion on the child she has borne?
> Though she may forget,
> I will not forget you!"
> See, I have engraved you on the palms of my hands."
> (Isaiah 49:14–16)

> "As a mother comforts her child,
> so I will comfort you;
> and you will be comforted over Jerusalem."
> (Isaiah 66:13)

Here, God the Father is comparing Himself not only to a mother, but to a nursing mother. In these words, He is expressing the kind of love that will rise up a thousand times in the night to care for her crying child. She will wait up until her child comes home and she knows they are safe in their bed. She will get up and tend to her children, even if she herself is unwell. She will forfeit her dinner just so her child will not go hungry. She will wake up early and make those school lunches. She will become her kid's Uber driver and take them all over the city to make sure they attend their extracurricular activities. She will brave the cold wind to watch her son play baseball and cheer him on in the ice-cold bleachers. She will endure the heat and humidity while watching her son play football. She will bake and cook their favorite meals just because she wants them to know they are loved.

You may be reading this with a pit in your stomach because your childhood was void of a mother who loved you in these ways. We are all born with an innate desire for a nurturing mother to take care of us. But even if you didn't have that growing up, the Lord still wants you to experience this kind of love. God the Father has the ability through the person of Holy Spirit to be the mother you never had.

What comes to mind when you think of Holy Spirit? If your immediate reaction is negative, that's okay. It's an indication of a wrong perspective and an invitation to allow Him to reveal the truth of who He really is. So much of our understanding of each *person* of the Trinity is influenced by our relationship (or lack thereof) with our earthly parents and siblings: mother, father, brother, or sister. Because, as humans, we're in an earthly experience while trying to commune with a supernatural God, we must be careful not to allow our limited *earthly* experience to dictate a *heavenly reality.* We often have a disconnected relationship with Holy Spirit when we have a dysfunctional relationship with our earthly mother.

In inner healing counseling, I often take people through the Father Ladder that I learned from the Sozo inner healing method at Grace Center in Franklin, Tennessee.[7] Typically, if there is a disconnect, fracture, or abuse from an earthly relationship, it affects our understanding and perception of how we see God. The understanding of each person of the Godhead—Father, Son, and Holy Spirit—is usually impacted negatively. When we present God the Father to someone, they will often view Him through the lens of what their relationship was like with their biological or adoptive father. A similar thing happens when Jesus is presented. He often represents the experience someone has had with their siblings or a close friend. Last, when presenting Holy Spirit, people often perceive Him through the lens of how their relationship was with their mother. Because our earthly realities are the only experiences we can pull from, we tend to impose those perspectives onto how we relate to each person of the Trinity.

We have access to the mother we all longed for through Holy Spirit, and we can become the mother that we never had to our children. We don't need to repeat the cycle of dysfunction. We can allow Holy Spirit to heal those areas in our lives, and as a result, we can comfort those around us because we have received comfort from Holy Spirit first. Even if you never had a mother who loved you in a nurturing, unconditional way, the Lord can show you how to extend that love to your children and to those around you.

God is a greater expression of motherhood than any human mother—even in the fullness of her nurturing nature. He is the original source and expression of motherhood. He has an infinitely greater capacity to comfort you and love you tenderly. Who better to reveal the nurturing side of Himself than the One who designed mothers? He is El Shaddai. He is God Almighty, and He is *everything* that you need.

> "But the Helper (Comforter, Advocate, Intercessor—Counselor, Strengthener, Standby), the Holy Spirit, whom the Father will send in My name [in My place, to represent Me and act on My behalf], He will teach you all things. And He will help you remember everything that I have told you." (John 14:26 AMP)

This is good news! No matter if you had the best mother or worst mother, God the Father has the ability to express the mother's heart you've always longed for.

Early on in my walk with God, there were times I felt insecure when approaching Him in prayer. I carried deep shame if I had not read my Bible every day. I thought that if I didn't practice spiritual disciplines on a daily basis, I had no right to access the person of Holy Spirit. I would often distance myself and feel guilty in asking for anything because deep down in my heart, my core belief system was a works-based relationship with God. I believed that if I did all the religious practices, then I'd be worthy enough to ask God for things in my prayer life. I had it so wrong! God is not keeping score with how much we perform for Him. His heart is that we desire to read the Word and spend time in worship—not because we *have* to but because we

God is not keeping score with how much we perform for Him.

get to. It is not our works that make us worthy to have a relationship with Holy Spirit, rather, it was the work of Jesus at the cross that made us worthy to enter His presence and receive from the Lord.

One day I was in a discipleship group with my pastors, and they were taking us through the Father Ladder, the inner healing model I explained earlier. Every person in my group, including myself, asked for prayer because we all had a distorted view of the Godhead. Even though I had a wonderful relationship with Holy Spirit from a young age, there was one area that always tripped me up. It had nothing to do with Holy Spirit Himself, but everything to do with how I saw my relationship with Him.

When I went into prayer with my pastor, Holy Spirit reminded me of an experience I had when I was a little girl. He showed me a picture in my mind—times when I had disappointed my mother by not doing the chores or something she had asked me to do. When that happened, my mum would give me the silent treatment for a day or two. I was always left wondering what I had done wrong and why she wasn't talking to me. Every time it happened, it felt like punishment. Holy Spirit then showed me that I had been believing a lie: If I didn't do what my mum required of me, I would be in trouble and get the silent treatment. Therefore, I assumed it must be the same when I approach Holy Spirit and felt like I had failed Him in some way.

When He showed me that picture, I began to weep in His presence. He was revealing to me that He didn't want a relationship based on works, but on unconditional love and acceptance. He showed me that being with Him should feel free and easy, like a friend sitting on a couch with no agenda, exchanging words and details about life. I wept and wept until the tears had run dry. After that session of prayer, I felt like a weight had been lifted off my shoulders.

Now I approach Holy Spirit in a personal way, even if I didn't pick up the Bible that day, because I have a deeper understanding of my relationship with Him. Communing with Him through worship or conversation is just as important as reading the Word and praying on a daily basis. He truly is my best friend now.

If you have ever felt condemned for not "doing enough" to please God, throw off that weight, shame, and guilt. The mother heart of Father God simply wants to dwell with you in an intimate, nurturing relationship. I guarantee that when the pressure comes off, you won't be able to stop communing with Him because you'll be approaching Him from a place of freedom, not striving from a place of obligation or duty.

Holy Spirit will meet you where you are and bring comfort to those places that need His personal ministry. I have discovered such a beautiful and intimate relationship with Holy Spirit—one that has nurtured, challenged, taught, and led me when no human had what I needed. I have had some of the most profound breakthroughs when I have brought my needs directly to the nurturing mother heart of God. Why don't you take a moment right now to close your eyes and pray the prayer below and allow Holy Spirit to reveal to you where the deficits are in your view of Him.

PRAYER

Holy Spirit, I come before You now and ask You to reveal where the wound began for me in having a dysfunctional relationship with my mother. I ask You to heal those areas that I carry from my childhood. I thank You for the gift of Your grace and the promise of restoration. Help me to release the pain and resentment that I have carried and open my heart to Your love and compassion for her. Help me see that she did not have the capacity to love me in the way I needed to be loved. Reveal any areas to me where I have held judgment against her and help me forgive her. I believe that You can help me to break free from unhealthy patterns I inherited. Grant me the strength to embrace my true worth and potential found in You. May Your peace fill my mind, Your love flood my heart, and my relationship with both You and my mother be reconciled in Jesus' name, amen.

CHAPTER 6

Being Baptized in the Holy Spirit

Jesus knew that to truly live this life here on earth and overcome the issues we face in our human experience, we would need supernatural power. We live in a fallen world that is decaying and disintegrating because of sin. In His love for us, Jesus understood that we couldn't fight these battles on our own, and that is why He instructed His disciples to *wait* for His power to come upon them. As a result of their obedience to His instruction, they experienced an explosion of power and became unstoppable in their faith.

In Acts 2, after Jesus instructed them not to leave Jerusalem until they had been given the gift the Father promised, the believers gathered in the upper room and waited to be clothed with power from on high. Everyone in that room had a supernatural experience with Holy Spirit. Tongues of fire rested on each of them, they were filled with Holy Spirit, and they all began to speak in other tongues. That same day, the apostle Peter stood before thousands of onlookers from many nations who were visiting Jerusalem on the day of Pentecost.

With boldness and power, Peter quoted the prophet Joel to explain what had just happened, saying, "And it shall come to pass in the last days, says God, that *I will pour out of My Spirit on all flesh*; your sons and your daughters shall prophesy, your young men shall see visions, your old men shall dream dreams" (Acts 2:17 NKJV, emphasis mine). The promise from Joel 2:22 was fulfilled that day. The Spirit of God was poured out on all flesh—on both sons *and* daughters—to empower all people to be God's witnesses throughout the earth. This supernatural power gave them the ability to fulfill the Great Commission: "Go and make disciples of all nations, baptizing them in the name of the Father and of the Son and of the Holy Spirit, and teaching them to obey everything I have commanded you. And surely I am with you always, to the very end of the age" (Matthew 28:19–20).

The news of what God was doing spread across the earth, and now, generations later, we are still living in the ripple effect of their bold witness. As believers, we need a personal revelation that we carry supernatural power to overcome anything that attempts to keep us from living victoriously. If we carry the same Spirit that raised Jesus from the dead, we must not settle for an ordinary existence, merely coping with life's struggles.

Holy Spirit's power is essential for every disciple to become an effective witness, enabling them to preach the gospel, perform miracles, experience a transformed life, and, ultimately, fulfill Jesus' command in the Great Commission. Beyond being witnesses, being baptized in Holy Spirit also empowers believers to experience a deeper relationship with God, receive spiritual gifts, be equipped for spiritual warfare, and walk boldly in their faith.

I shared my own Spirit baptism experience in chapter 2, but I have also witnessed thousands over the past thirty years experience this power in their walk with God. I will never forget witnessing my own daughter being supernaturally baptized during worship at church. She was eleven years old when Holy Spirit met her in a personal and beautiful way. There was no one around her or praying for her. In fact, she didn't even ask for it. The presence of God was so tangible in the meeting that she was simply overcome by Holy Spirit.

I remember she was sitting in the front row at church. As I stepped onto the stage to begin preaching, I heard an unusual sound coming from the left side of the building. I thought, *Who is this person crying out like that? It sounds like wailing and praying all at the same time.* As I looked over, I was stunned to see my daughter prostrate on the floor, tears streaming down her cheeks, and her mouth moving so rapidly it was as if the words were coming from the deepest parts of her. I knew something supernatural was happening.

I beckoned her to come, and as she made her way to the stage, I gently asked what was happening, but she could not speak any English. She kept praying in tongues and suddenly, the atmosphere became charged in a way that I can only describe as supernatural. It was as if the room became electrified—charged with the presence of God Almighty. The room was silent. Every eye in the congregation was fixed on her as she encountered the power of Holy Spirit baptizing her.

After a few moments, she began to speak in English. With tears in her eyes, she explained to the church what she was experiencing. She said she hadn't asked for this, but that when the Spirit of God came upon her, it felt like fire and oil pouring out over her. She was so overwhelmed that she could not stand up straight, and she felt the love of God in a way she had never experienced before.

As she was sharing, I sensed Holy Spirit telling me that I was to teach on being baptized in the Holy Spirit instead of preaching the message I had prepared. I listened and obeyed. I shared that what had happened to Holly was found in Scripture and extended an invitation to those who wanted to be filled. Over sixty people came forward that night and received the baptism of the Holy Spirit along with their prayer language at the altar. That was over ten years ago, and many people who are still a part of our church refer to that night as one of the most powerful and tangible experiences they've ever had in church.

This supernatural power has helped countless believers in their walk of faith—helped them overcome challenges and empowered them to do things for God they never thought possible. I truly believe that one day, when we're in heaven and speak with those who lived in Old Testament times, they will ask what it was like to have the Spirit of God dwelling within us and His power resting upon us. In the Old Testament, only a select group of kings, judges, and priests were given the privilege of Holy Spirit coming upon them for specific assignments. Not everyone had access to this power like we do today. I'm so thankful that Jesus left us the gift of His Spirit so we can access His power, peace, and presence every minute of every day!

God desires us to have this experience of power as soon as we come to Christ for salvation. This baptism enables us with "dunamis power." In the Greek, *dunamis* means power, efficiency, and might; a supernatural power given by God to live this life.[1] Let's look at how the apostle Paul explained this incredible reality:

> I pray that the eyes of your heart may be enlightened in order that you may know the hope to which he has called you, the riches of his glorious inheritance in his holy people, and his

> incomparably great power for us who believe. That power is the same as the mighty strength he exerted when he raised Christ from the dead and seated him at his right hand in the heavenly realms, far above all rule and authority, power and dominion, and every name that is invoked, not only in the present age but also in the one to come. And God placed all things under his feet and appointed him to be head over everything for the church. (Ephesians 1:18–22)

Paul helped us grasp the magnitude of God's power that's available to us in this passage. Harold W. Hoehner's commentary goes on to expound on this beautifully:

> The word "*power*" (*dynamis;* cf. 3:20) means a spiritually dynamic and living force. This power of God is directed toward believers. Paul then used three additional words to describe God's power. It is according to the working (*energeian*, "energetic power," from which comes the English "energy") of the might (*kratous*, "power that overcomes resistance," as in Christ's miracles; this word is used only of God, never of believers) of God's inherent strength (*ischyos*) which He provides (cf. 6:10; 1 Peter 4:11). This magnificent accumulation of words for power underscores the magnitude of God's "great power" available to Christians.[2]

Baptism means to dip, immerse, submerge, or overwhelm.[3] When you experience being baptized in Holy Spirit, you are fully submerged in the Spirit of God in the same way you would be submerged in water during a water baptism (Matthew 3:15–16; Acts 1:5). This experience is an endowment with power from on high (Acts 1:8). It is a seal—a mark or sign of ownership by Holy Spirit (Ephesians 1:13). It is a down payment and a guarantee of our future inheritance and redemption when we are free of death and sin (Ephesians 1:13–14). Last, it is a gift—Holy Spirit is a gift from Christ to us (John 16:7).

I remember the first time I heard the "cucumber becoming a pickle" analogy, and it's stuck with me ever since. This example is often used to explain being baptized in Holy Spirit because it highlights the transformation that occurs when a person is immersed in God's presence, power, and teachings. Just as a cucumber undergoes a significant change when submerged in brine and becomes something entirely new—a pickle—a believer experiences a spiritual metamorphosis when immersed in God's Spirit.

The work and functions of Holy Spirit are many and varied, but all with one goal: to conform each one of us to the image of Christ. The Holy Spirit works in our lives to produce the fruit of the Spirit, which reflects the quality of His character and nature. Being baptized in Holy Spirit, however, is for the purpose of producing power and supernatural abilities so we can be effective workers in His kingdom. The Lord gives us spiritual gifts, such as the power to heal the sick, raise the dead, and bring forth deliverance to those who are oppressed. These divine empowerments are not only meant to strengthen us but also to serve others. This is not just a one-time event but an ongoing journey of growth and transformation. We have been commissioned to make disciples of all nations, but when we're consumed by our own pain and personal issues, we lose the motivation to look outward and see the needs of others.

I truly believe that this is the Enemy's plan: to keep humanity powerless and stuck in their issues so they become ineffective witnesses to the world around them. When this happens on a larger scale, the church becomes a sleeping giant that's silent, stagnant, and carries no power. This is the antithesis of what Jesus Christ died to give us! Paul said, "But you will receive *power* when the Holy Spirit comes on you; and you will be my witnesses in Jerusalem, and in all Judea and Samaria, and to the ends of the earth" (Acts 1:8, emphasis mine).

> Being baptized in Holy Spirit, however, is for the purpose of producing power and supernatural abilities so we can be effective workers in His kingdom.

There is no greater power than the Spirit of God working in our lives, and there is no substitute for the presence of the Holy Spirit. It is a real, definitive experience, a biblical experience, and an identifiable experience, accompanied by physical and spiritual evidence (Acts 2:4, 33). You know if and when you receive it. Others standing by know it too. It brings a deeper relationship with God and a transformation of character, enabling us to grow in holiness and live according to God's will.

PROOF IN THE GOSPELS

This concept of being baptized in the Holy Spirit is not just for the charismatic Christian. This truth is written in the Bible, and we need to make sure we study the Word of God before assuming it is just a preference. There is proof in Scripture that shows us that being baptized in Holy Spirit is necessary in our walk with God. I hope that as you see the evidence throughout this chapter, you will understand that every Christian should desire this gift. John the Baptist said that Jesus Christ would baptize His followers "with the Holy Spirit and with fire" (Luke 3:16 RSV). Jesus repeated this when He declared, "For John baptized with water, but before many days you shall be baptized with the Holy Spirit" (Acts 1:5 RSV). Jesus used another phrase to describe this same experience, telling His disciples to wait "until you are endued with power from on high" (Luke 24:49 NKJV).

John the Baptist was considered the greatest prophet, according to Jesus. He likened him to Elijah, the great prophet in the Old Testament. Yet Jesus said, "Truly I tell you, among those born of women there has not risen anyone greater than John the Baptist; yet whoever is least in the kingdom of heaven is greater than he" (Matthew 11:11). What does this mean? How can the least of these in the new kingdom of God be greater than John the Baptist? William Barclay helped explain this beautiful mystery:

> But what was it that John lacked? What is it that the Christian has that John could never have? The answer is simple and fundamental. *John had never seen the cross.* Therefore, one thing John could never know—the full revelation of the love of God. The holiness of God he might know; the justice of God he might declare; but the love of God in all its fullness he could never know.[4]

This also means that John never experienced the resurrection power of Jesus or the outpouring of Holy Spirit. I believe that if John were alive today, he would say to us, "Do you realize what you have access to? The person and power of Holy Spirit, the same Spirit that raised Jesus from the dead, lives in you. Use freely the power He has gifted you and you will do even greater things than we did while here on earth!"

PROOF IN THE BOOK OF ACTS

There is also clear evidence in the book of Acts where we see numerous accounts of people being baptized in Holy Spirit, further showing that it is necessary for us today.

> "For John baptized with water, but in a few days you will be baptized with the Holy Spirit." (1:5)

> All of them were filled with the Holy Spirit and began to speak in other tongues as the Spirit enabled them. (2:4)

> After they prayed, the place where they were meeting was shaken. And they were all filled with the Holy Spirit and spoke the word of God boldly. (4:31)

> When they arrived, they prayed for the new believers there that they might receive the Holy Spirit, because the Holy Spirit had not yet come on any of them; they had simply been baptized in the name of the Lord Jesus. Then Peter and John placed their hands on them, and they received the Holy Spirit. (8:15–17)

> The circumcised believers who had come with Peter were astonished that the gift of the Holy Spirit had been poured out even on Gentiles. For they heard them speaking in tongues and praising God. (10:45–46)

> When Paul placed his hands on them, the Holy Spirit came on them, and they spoke in tongues and prophesied. (19:6)

TO WHOM DID GOD PROMISE THIS EXPERIENCE?

Throughout my journey as a pastor, I have heard many people say that they don't need to be baptized in Holy Spirit. While Spirit baptism is not imperative for your salvation, why would you settle for less when Jesus paid the price for us to walk in supernatural power? Upon experiencing being baptized in Holy Spirit, you're brought into a supernatural realm and grow in authority as a believer.

It is a powerful tool you can access at any time to help you overcome life's greatest challenges. We need the power of Holy Spirit to guide, empower, and transform us, enabling us to live a life that reflects God's love and truth. We cannot do this in our own strength. It is the Spirit who helps us understand Scripture, empowers us to overcome sin, and gives us the strength to live a godly life.

We need the power of Holy Spirit to break strongholds in our lives. We fight against powers of darkness from the position of Jesus overcoming death and declaring victory at the cross. Even though we are saved while living here on earth, we also have a real Enemy who seeks to steal, kill, and destroy us. His mission is to keep us bound here on earth so that we struggle through life instead of thriving. We need the authority that Jesus has given to us to fight the spiritual battles that come our way.

God doesn't play favorites or reserve His gifts for only a

select few. The invitation is open to everyone. Romans 2:11 says, "God shows no partiality" (ESV). Scripture tells us that all we need to do is ask the Father and He will give us Holy Spirit (Luke 11:13). He wants all of us to have this free gift.

> We need the power of Holy Spirit to break strongholds in our lives.

> Peter replied, "Repent and be baptized, every one of you, in the name of Jesus Christ for the forgiveness of your sins. And you will receive the gift of the Holy Spirit. The promise is for you and your children and for all who are far off—for all whom the Lord our God will call." (Acts 2:38–39)

Let's break this scripture down to see who God has freely given the gift of Holy Spirit to:

- The present generation—"for you and your children"
- All Gentile believers—"for all who are far off"
- All—"for all whom the Lord our God will call"

Yes, He promised this gift to *all* who would believe. That means you! He promised to give *you* this wonderful, supernatural experience.

EVIDENCE THROUGH THE GIFT OF TONGUES

According to Scripture, many people, upon experiencing being baptized in Holy Spirit, began to speak in tongues. While some people believe in this gift, others struggle to accept the gift of speaking in tongues. Scripture clearly shows us that *all* believers have access to this experience through Holy Spirit.

Jesus said, "Whoever believes and is baptized will be saved, but whoever does not believe will be condemned. And these signs will accompany those who believe: In my name they will drive out demons; they will speak in new tongues" (Mark 16:16–17). Speaking in tongues is not the measurement of someone's spiritual development. It is a gift and has nothing to do with any degree of spiritual growth, small or great. Just as salvation is not earned by our goodness but received as a free gift, so is the gift of speaking in tongues.

It is possible, however, to receive Holy Spirit without speaking in tongues at first. I have met many people who are filled with Holy Spirit but did not immediately speak in tongues. Their prayer language was released later. There are times when it can take a while for this gift to manifest in our lives, but don't give up easily or resolve that it will never happen. It is a divine gift; therefore, God wants us to have it even more than we desire it.

We must understand that we receive this gift by *faith*, rather than trying to work it out with our intellect. I have seen many people receive this gift even after asking God for it several times in the past. Receiving the gift of speaking in tongues is not a matter of *if* it will happen, but rather *when* it will happen. It is not possible to be baptized by the Holy Spirit and *not* have the *ability* to speak in tongues. When we receive Holy Spirit, we receive all that He is, which means we can access all His spiritual gifts, and that includes speaking in tongues.

I have heard it described like this: If I were to give you a

Swiss Army knife and you received it, you would have access to everything it offers. You could use as little or as much of that Swiss Army knife as you wanted to. You may not use the blade or the spoon right away, but you still have the ability to use them if you choose. Sometimes, when Holy Spirit fills us, we have so many hesitations about tongues that we choose to forfeit the gift altogether. But this doesn't mean you don't have Holy Spirit—you do. You still have the Spirit of God within you. All you have to do is ask, by faith, and allow the gift God has given you to begin flowing out of your mouth. People make it seem like operating in this gift is complicated, but in reality, it's very simple. We need to be in a posture of surrender, yielding ourselves and allowing God's Spirit to come upon us.

The challenge is so many of us want to be in control. We don't want to yield our minds, bodies, and spirits to God because we like being in the driver's seat. This need for control is often rooted in unresolved trauma and unhealed pain. People who have experienced negative situations outside of their control often cope by developing an incessant need for control. However, Holy Spirit, as your Divine Counselor, wants to bring healing to those areas of your life—but it starts with submitting to His lordship and surrendering to His way.

This is why it can be difficult for those who are more left-brained, analytical, and logic-driven to receive their spirit language. They often approach this experience as something to understand or learn cognitively, like trying to learn a new language. But speaking in tongues isn't learned through the mind—it's a spiritual experience where Jesus baptizes you in Holy Spirit and immerses you with His Spirit. The key to receiving this gift is releasing control and allowing the Spirit of God to move. When we yield our control and our mind to the Lord, He baptizes us supernaturally.

The overflow of being filled with the Spirit comes from your innermost belly and bubbles up out of your mouth, not from your brain and then out of your mouth. That is why when you are baptized and begin to speak in other tongues, it can feel as if your tongue is moving faster than normal without your control. Some of you reading this right now might feel uncomfortable when I say, "without your control." This is key though. It's only when we surrender ourselves to God and invite Him to baptize us that we give Him permission to overwhelm us in the best possible way.

WHY SHOULD WE SPEAK IN TONGUES?

There are many other powerful benefits to speaking in tongues. Let's break down a few.

1. It Edifies Us

Paul revealed that "anyone who speaks in a tongue edifies themselves" (1 Corinthians 14:4). *Edify* means to instruct or uplift someone in a way that enlightens them spiritually, intellectually, or morally. It also means to build up; to charge as with a battery; to make strong.[5] Paul also told the church to "be filled with the Spirit, speaking to one another with psalms, hymns, and songs from the Spirit. Sing and make music from your heart to the Lord" (Ephesians 5:18–19). Another passage that emphasizes this says, "But you, dear friends, by building yourselves up in your most holy faith, and praying in the Holy Spirit, keep yourselves in God's love as you wait for the mercy of our Lord Jesus Christ to bring you to eternal life" (Jude vv. 20–21).

Praying in the Spirit is a powerful weapon against the Enemy when we're feeling overwhelmed and anxious. Anytime I feel overwhelm creeping in, I begin to pray in the Spirit, and it is amazing how my mind submits to the supernatural power of God that flows over me as I speak. Sometimes the only way I can shake off sadness, worry, or anxiety is by praying in the Spirit. When I do, it supernaturally builds my faith, and I leave better than I entered that prayer time.

Praying in the Spirit is like filling up our fuel tank so we can maintain our strength in our walk of faith. Paul proclaimed he did it more than anyone! (1 Corinthians 14:18). He also said, "I would like every one of you to speak in tongues" (v. 5). Imagine if every time you felt the urge to talk through your issues with someone, you began to pray instead. It truly does make a difference! The next time you find yourself feeling anxious, why don't you try casting your cares on the Divine Counselor?

2. It Improves Our Communication with God

> For anyone who speaks in a tongue does not speak to people but to God. Indeed, no one understands them; they utter mysteries by the Spirit. (1 Corinthians 14:2)

Speaking in tongues helps us with our direct communication with God. Through this gift, we can communicate directly to God from our spirit to His Spirit. Even though we live in an earthly body, God created us as a spirit man first. Our physical body is connected to this earth, but our spirit is what connects to God in the supernatural realm. When we pray in tongues, our spirit speaks directly to God's Spirit, bypassing the human mind and will.

I have found that when I pray in tongues, my spirit is engaged with His Spirit. Often, after a few minutes, thoughts in my native language will come to my mind—thoughts I had not been thinking about prior to my prayer time. I often write those thoughts down, and it has proven incredibly fruitful over the years. As I pray in the Spirit—speaking words that seem unintelligible—God begins to drop thoughts from His heart into my spirit. I then act on those promptings and watch as God moves in powerful ways.

For example, a picture of someone's face will pop into my mind's eye as I'm praying. I will write that name down and then call them to ask if everything is okay. Many times, that person needed prayer or encouragement right in that moment. God revealed that by His Spirit so I could help somebody in their time of need. I've also seen the Lord do the same for me. When my heart is heavy and I don't know what to pray, He will impress something specific on my heart, or He will shift my perspective. I am then able to tackle that particular situation with a strategy that brings peace and clarity, instead of living in constant chaos in my mind and heart about it.

3. We Share in Divine Mysteries and Secrets

One of the most beautiful aspects to speaking in tongues is that we get to share divine mysteries and secrets. People who are ignorant of the value of speaking in tongues often say it's just "empty gibberish." Scripture says that speaking in tongues is sharing mysteries or secrets with God in the Spirit (1 Corinthians 14:2). That sounds far removed from gibberish!

Through the Spirit, the believer speaking in tongues rises into a supernatural realm of revelation—a realm where God unfolds His secret mysteries. By faith, the humblest Christian speaking in tongues is uttering secrets that are far beyond the mind of the greatest scholar. And the best news is that the Enemy has no understanding of what is being said. So, when we pray in the Spirit, he can't twist the truth or distort it with lies because he doesn't understand it at all!

I have personally discovered powerful revelation in the Word of God after praying in tongues. It feels like a bright spotlight highlights a particular passage of Scripture and the Lord downloads a fresh revelation into my spirit that changes everything. God shares His secrets with friends, not simply acquaintances. In the same way we share deep, personal secrets only to those who are closest to us, the Lord operates the same way. He "confides in those who fear him; he makes his covenant known to them" (Psalm 25:14). Oh, what a privilege it is to share secrets with God our Father through the work of Holy Spirit revealing them to us!

4. We Worship and Praise God

> They heard them speaking in tongues and praising God. (Acts 10:46)

When we pray in the Spirit, we are also praising God. Acts 2:6 says, "Each one heard their own language being spoken." My friend Paul recently shared a story about a prayer meeting in Australia that his brother Russell was leading. When the meeting finished, a lady came up to him and asked if he was aware that he was speaking in Aramaic. She told him that she spoke several languages and that he had glorified God in Aramaic and prayed for mercy on our land in Hebrew. It blessed her tremendously to see this gift in operation today.

Every time we speak in tongues through faith, we get a larger view of God—His greatness, His love, His power, and all He encompasses. No one can make God bigger than He already is, but when we speak in tongues through worship and praise, we magnify Him with our spirits, and He looms greater in our lives. You can speak and worship God in this wonderful language He has supernaturally given to you whether you're in the bedroom, the kitchen, the garden, the shower, or the car. It is not reserved for Sunday church services or when you feel polished and put together. Anywhere and everywhere, His Spirit is with you! When you constantly commune with the Lord in this supernatural way, you will find His presence becomes even more tangible to you. What a beautiful gift He has given to all of us!

THE SCIENCE OF SPEAKING IN TONGUES

Brain specialist Carl Peterson conducted a study in 2011, researching the relationship between praying or speaking in tongues (glossolalia) and the brain. The study found that as people worship or pray, the brain releases two chemicals, boosting the immune system by 35 to 40 percent. These chemicals are directed from a part of the brain that is only activated by Spirit-led prayer and worship.[6]

Another study examined stress levels in Pentecostals by measuring cortisol and alpha-amylase from saliva samples. The samples were collected on Sundays and Mondays to compare stress levels on worship and nonworship days. The study found that speaking in tongues results in reduced stress levels and significantly increases calmness and enhances mood.[7] This isn't just scientific, it's scriptural!

The University of Pennsylvania School of Medicine conducted a study on what happens physiologically to the brain when a person speaks in tongues. Principal researcher Andrew Newberg made the following comments about their findings:

> We noticed a number of changes that occurred functionally in the brain. Our finding of decreased activity in the frontal lobes during the practice of speaking in tongues is fascinating because these subjects truly believe that the spirit of God is moving through them and controlling them to speak. Our brain imaging research shows us that these subjects are not in control of the usual language centers during this activity, which is consistent with their description of a lack of intentional control while speaking in tongues. These findings could be interpreted as the subject's sense of self being taken over by something else. We, scientifically, assume it is being taken over by another part of the brain, but we could not see, in this imaging study, where this took place. We believe this is the first scientific imaging study evaluating changes in cerebral activity—looking at what happens to the brain—when someone is speaking in tongues. This study also showed a number of other changes in the brain, including those areas involved in emotions and establishing our sense of self.[8]

I love it when science confirms what we already know through Scripture. When scientific discoveries align with biblical truths, it can reinforce the belief that God's Word is true and reliable to those who need proof to believe.

WE SHOULD CONSTANTLY BE FILLED WITH THE SPIRIT

> Therefore do not be foolish, but understand what the Lord's will is. Do not get drunk on wine, which leads to debauchery. Instead, be filled with the Spirit. (Ephesians 5:17–18)

Scripture also teaches us that we must be *continually* filled with Holy Spirit. Acts 4:31 says, "After they prayed, the place where they were meeting was shaken. And they were all filled with the Holy Spirit and spoke the Word of God boldly." These apostles and believers had already been filled with the Spirit on the day of Pentecost, but they needed constant refilling to maintain the power of God. In the same way, we need to be constantly filled with the Holy Spirit so He can empower us to live a life of purpose, strength, and guidance. Think of it as a bottle of water that gets emptied as we sip it all day. At the end of the day, that water bottle needs a refilling so we can continue to drink from it and refresh our bodies physically. We need this refilling spiritually. By engaging with His presence on a daily basis and asking Holy Spirit to fill us up as we pour out each day to help ourselves and others, He can provide His power to overcome adversity, experience joy, and live out God's calling.

If you would like to be baptized in the Holy Spirit but don't have anyone to pray for you, I'd love to pray with you. Simply scan the QR code and it will take you to a video where I share how you can be filled with Holy Spirit, right where you are. But first, let's finish this chapter with a prayer to ask Him to baptize you with His Spirit.

PRAYER

Dear Jesus, I desire to be baptized in Holy Spirit, and I am asking You to fill me. Will You unlock my prayer language as I open my heart to receive this gift You have promised? If there is any doubt in me, I ask You to fill it with faith and I ask You to baptize me in the Holy Spirit. Fill me with Your supernatural power so I can exercise this gift in my everyday life. In Jesus' name, amen.

CHAPTER 7

The Divine Power to Overcome Strongholds

When I first moved to Nashville, I met many believers who thought their issues in life were impossible to overcome. They would flock to the altars after every service asking me to pray for them. Of course, I gladly helped where I could, but I realized that many of these beautiful men and women did not have the understanding that the very issues they were coming to me about could be overcome if they understood the power that lived inside them. I realized that many of these people were not equipped with the knowledge that believers have divine power to pull down the strongholds in their lives that keep them bound.

The Bible clearly explains this:

> For though we live in the world, we do not wage war as the world does. The weapons we fight with are not the weapons of the world. On the contrary, they have divine power to demolish strongholds. We demolish arguments and every pretension that sets it itself up against the knowledge of God, and we take captive every thought to make it obedient to Christ. And we will be ready to punish every act of disobedience, once your obedience is complete. (2 Corinthians 10:3–6)

But what does this look like in our everyday life? How does the Divine Counselor lead us through this process? Let's go deeper together.

WHAT IS A STRONGHOLD?

At its core, a stronghold is a yoke of bondage that keeps you imprisoned and hinders you from living the abundant life Christ died to give you. Strongholds are always strategies from the Enemy with the primary purpose of keeping you in destructive and damaging cycles of behavior. They can come in many forms of emotional baggage. They can also manifest as unforgiveness, which then wreaks havoc on our minds and hearts. Bitterness and unforgiveness are like cancer in our bodies. They rob us of authority and power and ultimately make us spiritually sick. Whatever holds us back from truly living in freedom and experiencing an abundant life is a stronghold. To put it plainly: A stronghold is anything that has a choke hold on you and won't let go.

What types of strongholds limit us in our life? What really keeps us from living in the freedom and fullness that God designed for us to experience? There are various kinds of strongholds that we've all struggled with. I believe these seven, however, have caused the most bondage in the body of Christ: fear, unforgiveness, anxiety, depression, anger, shame, and addiction.

Strongholds are fueled by the lies of the Enemy. The Enemy will stop at nothing to deceive you because his goal is to destroy you. His primary tactic is to convince you that the lies he feeds you are truth. Satan is the father of lies, and through his lies, he deceives you into thinking wrong thoughts about yourself, your situation, and other people around you. He locates a vulnerable area in your heart—a past trauma, a failure, or a personal weakness—and shoots a fiery dart into that place. If you take the bait and believe him, these lies distort your ability to walk and live in the fullness of your salvation.

According to Scripture, "There is no truth in him. When he lies, he speaks his native language" (John 8:44). The Enemy will also use accusations to paralyze us. Revelation tells us that Satan is "the accuser of our brethren" (12:10 NKJV). He relentlessly reminds you of your past sins and failures. When you listen and meditate on those accusations, guilt, shame, and condemnation set in. When we make agreements with the Enemy's lies over our life, we give him power over us—power to control our thoughts and emotions. This is how he gains ground in our thought life.

A stronghold begins in the mind—often as a sinful thought, belief, attitude, or desire—and then becomes a lived experience or habit. This habit shapes a core belief, which then forms a distorted truth—one that has a demonic attachment because you made an agreement with a lie. When we believe the lies of the Enemy, they begin to form a belief system that affects our behavior and becomes a pattern of living that takes over our lives. These distorted belief systems are based on falsehood, and they have tremendous power to affect our feelings and emotions (our heart and soul).

Many Christians feel guilt-ridden and worthless because of incorrect thinking. They feel unloved, unaccepted, unworthy, inferior, sinful, broken, hopeless, and like they don't belong. Their perception of God the Father has been damaged due to past experiences and because they've internalized the Enemy's lies as their identity. This causes people to see God as a distant, disinterested, and grueling taskmaster—ready to condemn and punish—instead of as the loving, good Father that He truly is. This is the battlefield that goes on in our minds. If you've ever experienced the inner war that makes you toss and turn and immediately think of the worst-case scenario on a consistent basis, then you're probably struggling with a stronghold.

In order to overcome, we must first be aware of how the Enemy operates in our lives. Satan will use strongholds to keep you from living at full capacity. Even though you'll get to heaven because you are saved, you will struggle to live life here on earth. If you are living with anything that is holding you captive, then you are living beneath how God created you. He has grace for you—to walk this journey and also to live in freedom. Second Corinthians 3:17 says, "Now the Lord is the Spirit, and where the Spirit of the Lord is, there is freedom."

Paul wrote, "May God himself, the God of peace, sanctify you through and through. May your whole spirit, soul and body be kept blameless at the coming of our Lord Jesus Christ" (1 Thessalonians 5:23). God wants your body and soul to be in freedom, not just your spirit. We must walk out our salvation in Christ and allow the Word of God to renew our minds.

Even though our sins are forgiven, many of us have been living with bad habits through wrong thinking. This is what needs to change. The truth is, when you receive salvation, you become a new creation in Christ, but the journey doesn't stop there. It then becomes your responsibility to renew your mind so that your life can be transformed.

The Enemy's goal is for you to conform to the patterns of this world. This was my story. I was saved when I was eleven years old, but over the years my thinking had to change. What happened to me as a child caused me to believe at the core of my being that I was unlovable, unworthy of love, and a reject. This deep-seated belief did not disappear at salvation. My sin was forgiven, but then I had to unlearn the destructive thought patterns that kept me bound for years with an eating disorder addiction.

Because I believed for so long that I was unworthy and stupid, I made decisions that reinforced that lie until it became my truth. I would hear the preacher affirm, "God loves you," and yet I would inherently believe that He loves everyone else, but He tolerates me. I would think, *He has to love me because the Bible says so, but I don't feel like He loves me. If He loved me, then why did He allow these bad things to happen to me?* That was the core lie I believed: If God really loved me, He would have stopped any negative experience from happening to me.

The problem with that type of thinking is that it doesn't acknowledge that we live in a broken world full of sin. All have fallen short of the glory of God, and bad things happen to good people because of the sinful nature in people. God does not stop free will. Each person has the will to choose to do right or wrong on this earth, and unfortunately, many choose to do wrong to innocent people. This is the very reason Jesus came to earth—to destroy the works of the Evil One, so that we could be made whole again.

His Word promises that despite the negative things we endure, He makes all things beautiful, He works all things together for our good, and He takes what the Enemy meant to harm us with and turns it into our testimony. Our thought life makes all the difference. And for most of us, we rely on how we *feel* instead of on the *truth* of God's Word. Every feeling we have begins with a thought. This is why the Bible talks so much about guarding our hearts and minds. If we're not careful, we'll allow mind monsters to creep in and before we know it, we're spiraling emotionally, our lives feel out of control, and we don't feel God's nearness anymore. It all traces back to one thing: a thought you never took captive. What you *think* about determines how you *feel*. We must change our thinking if we want our lives to change.

> Finally, brothers and sisters, whatever is true, whatever is noble, whatever is right, whatever is pure, whatever is lovely, whatever is admirable—if anything is excellent or praiseworthy—*think* about such things. Whatever you have learned or received or heard from me, or seen in me—put it into practice. And the God of peace will be with you. (Philippians 4:8–9, emphasis mine)

Just as our bodies need nourishment and can be healed by eating clean, healthy foods instead of toxic, processed ones, our minds function the same way. The saying, "you are what you eat," rings true for both your physical body and your mental reality. When you feed on toxic thoughts, you meditate on negativity, and in turn, your attitude becomes negative, which can lead to oppression.

We must change our thinking if we want our lives to change.

OPPRESSION VS. POSSESSION

As a pastor, I've had many people ask me about demonic activity, so I want to bring some clarity to this area. Oppression and possession are two different things. For someone to be possessed, they must willingly give control to a demonic spirit. There has to be an open door or an invitation for the devil to come in and take possession of a person. The only way the devil can possess you is if you give him the power to do it. A Christian who has confessed with their mouth and believed in their heart that Jesus Christ is Lord, and that God raised Him from the dead, cannot be possessed by a demon because Jesus Christ lives inside them. They *can,* however, be oppressed by demonic spirits such as worry, fear, anxiety, and torment.

The *Merriam-Webster Dictionary* defines *oppress* as "to crush or burden by abuse of power or authority" or "to burden spiritually or mentally: weigh heavily upon."[1] Since the definition of oppression is an abuse of power or authority, we should ask, Who gives the devil authority to come in and oppress us? The only person who can empower the devil is you! God has given you free will, and you have the choice to open the door when the devil knocks. You can open the door to him either knowingly in rebellion, or unknowingly in ignorance because you were never taught. Regardless, you are the one who allows the devil to hijack and take residence in your mind and, consequently, abuse your thoughts and torment your emotions. When you make an agreement with the Enemy's lies, you give him power over you. To break this you need to come out of agreement with the lies he speaks and ask Jesus to forgive you for believing what is contrary to what God says about you.

> For though we live in the world, we do not wage war as the world does. The weapons we fight with are not the weapons of the world. On the contrary, they *have divine power to demolish strongholds.* We demolish arguments and every pretension

> [a claim or assertion of a claim to something] that sets itself up against the knowledge of God, and we take captive every thought to make it obedient to Christ. And we will be ready to punish every act of disobedience, once your obedience is complete. (2 Corinthians 10:3–6, emphasis mine)

As Paul explained, we are not fighting a physical war but rather a spiritual one. Warfare is the engagement in or the activities involved in war or conflict. Spiritual warfare is a battle that goes on in our minds between error and truth. If we are not equipped as saints, we will be overcome by the Enemy's plans, tactics, and weapons that he uses against us.

This is why we need to understand who our real enemy is and how he operates—so we can receive a divine strategy to overcome him. We don't have to live in fear that the Enemy is always after us because Jesus has given us the keys to win every battle! The Bible clearly says: "Then you will know the truth, and the truth will set you free" (John 8:32). You may be wondering, *How does the truth set us free?* How do we utilize the weapons Paul spoke about in 2 Corinthians 10 to break strongholds? Let's break this down.

HOW DO WE DEMOLISH STRONGHOLDS?

1. Read and Obey the Word of God

> All Scripture is God-breathed and is useful for teaching, rebuking, correcting and training in righteousness, so that the servant of God may be thoroughly equipped for every good work. (2 Timothy 3:16–17)

As Christians, we must believe the Bible is God-breathed and the final authority in our lives. When you read the Bible, *how* do you read it? Do you read it as God's love letter to you, revealing His heart and purpose? Do you read it as a blueprint from God that helps you understand how to live and respond to circumstances in your life? Do you read it to check off your devotional box of daily Bible reading? Or do you absorb what it is saying, and more important, do you obey its instruction?

> For the word of God is alive and active. Sharper than any double-edged sword, it penetrates even to dividing soul and spirit, joints and marrow; it judges the thoughts and attitudes of the heart. Nothing in all creation is hidden from God's sight. Everything is uncovered and laid bare before the eyes of him to whom we must give account. (Hebrews 4:12–13)

We cannot hide from God. He knows all things, and He is like a master surgeon using the scalpel of the Spirit to cut through to the deepest places and remove anything that is causing harm. He is so skillful and precise that the Word of God can read our souls, impart wisdom, and download revelation into our spirit, causing lasting change. If the Word of God is alive and active, it means it is constantly revealing areas in our lives that need pruning in order for growth and lasting change to happen. He will lead us in all truth if we study His Word not because we must, but because in it lies the freedom and transformation we need. The Word of God helps us with the issues we face daily, and when absorbed and applied, it influences us for the greater good.

A study performed by the Center for Bible Engagement compiled findings on the benefits of Christians reading their Bible. The statistics revealed shocking results for those who read the Word four times a week: Loneliness went down 30 percent, anger went down 32 percent, bitterness went down 40 percent, alcoholism went down 47 percent, feeling spiritually dead went down 60 percent, and watching porn went down 60 percent.[2]

This is incredible! You cannot tell me that the Bible doesn't change you if you are absorbing its contents. It does have the power to renew your mind, transform your life, and conform you to the likeness of Christ. It is our job to make reading it a priority and to choose to be led by God's Word, which was written by the Holy Spirit.

2. Pray and Worship

In addition to reading and obeying the Word of God, we must also pursue prayer and worship, especially when we don't *feel* like it. The moments we don't want to are exactly when we need to exercise that spiritual muscle the most. When we complain about our issues or criticize problems, we are giving in to what the Enemy wants us to do. When we choose to worship and pray in times of difficulty, however, it is like incense to the Lord, and it shifts the atmosphere of our heart and mind from defeat to victory. The best part is when we worship and pray in *faith*, even when we don't *feel* like it, it is like kryptonite to the Enemy. It debilitates him from having any power over us. Even though our circumstances may not immediately change, we change on the inside, and that is where strongholds are broken. As my husband says, "Praise precedes the miracle."

3. Replace the Lie with the Truth

We demolish strongholds by demolishing arguments. Let me explain. We demolish arguments by having a better argument that wins the battle. When the Enemy has power over your thought life, he floods your mind with his incessant accusation. This often sounds like: *You will never be good enough. You're a failure. Your situation is hopeless. Why don't you just give up? You're a fraud. You're damaged goods. You are unworthy.* And the list goes on. The only way you will overcome this attack is by using a stronger word that comes from God's Word. You need a stronger argument, as Paul Bergin said in *The Path of Presence*:

> If you want to fight an argument in the court of law, then you will need a more convincing argument—a truthful argument. In the battle of the spirit, we use THE WORD to fight words. We use the truth of Jesus and His Word to overcome the lies. Satan is known as the father of all lies (John 8:44). We, as disciples, don't look to our past. That argument finds us guilty, and that is why we cannot fight the enemy by ourselves. Mustering up your own willpower and positive thinking won't win out in a spiritual fight. We must look to our position in Christ. His word over us triumphs over any accusation of the enemy because the accounts of our old sinful nature are paid for by the blood of Jesus.[3]

Satan's strategy against us has been the same since the beginning of time. He tried to engage Adam and Eve in the garden through an argument, and he's still using the same tactic today with God's people. He doesn't have any new tricks up his sleeve. We were never meant to engage in an argument with the Enemy;

we're simply called to speak the truth of God's Word, which defeats every argument and pulls down every pretension that sets itself up against the knowledge of God.

When we don't know what the Word of God says, we end up arguing with the Enemy in our own strength or we believe what he says about us and are overcome by his tactics. Our responsibility is to demolish every accusation from the Enemy with God's truth, but we must know His Word to do this. Hosea 4:6 says, "My people are destroyed from lack of knowledge." The Hebrew word used here for "knowledge" is *da'ath*, which implies an intimate, experiential understanding rather than just factual information.[4] We must know the knowledge of His Word through revelation to fight the strongholds that try to take over our lives.

Strongholds are built on error, but they are torn down by truth. What does this mean? We take the error—the lie and accusation of the Enemy against us—and we replace it with the truth that comes from the Word of God. Then we declare the Word. There is power in speaking and praying Scripture out loud. Let's look at some common examples of how this works.

Strongholds are built on error, but they are torn down by truth.

Error: Look at your past; you should be ashamed of yourself.

Truth: The blood of Jesus washed you clean.

> As far as the east is from the west,
> so far has he removed our transgressions from us.
> (Psalm 103:12)

> "Come now. Let us settle the matter,"
> says the Lord.
> "Though your sins are like scarlet,
> they shall be as white as snow;
> though they are red like crimson,
> they shall be like wool."
> (Isaiah 1:18)

Error: You don't belong.
Truth: You've been adopted and accepted into the family of God.

> But you belong to God, my dear children. You have already won a victory over those people, because the Spirit who lives in you is greater than the spirit who lives in the world. (1 John 4:4 NLT)

Error: You're a mistake.
Truth: God created you on purpose, for a purpose.

> God created mankind in his own image. (Genesis 1:27)

> I praise you because I am fearfully and wonderfully made;
> your works are wonderful,
> I know that full well.
> (Psalm 139:14)

This is why it is important that we work together with Holy Spirit to demolish every stronghold that tries to keep us bound while we are here on earth. The degree to which we cooperate with Holy Spirit is the degree to which we will grow into the character of Jesus. The fruit of the Spirit begins to grow in our lives as we submit and surrender to the work of Holy Spirit within us. Even the challenges and hardships we face provide powerful opportunities for His fruit to be displayed through us. The fruit of the Spirit is love, joy, peace, patience, kindness, goodness, faithfulness, gentleness, and self-control (Galatians 5:22–23). Bearing fruit will not happen overnight though. It's a process of sanctification that takes time, intentionality, and discipline. We have to be fully committed to allowing Holy Spirit to show us the areas in our heart that need tending. Through His loving conviction, He will continually help us become more transformed into the image of Christ.

The degree to which we cooperate with Holy Spirit is the degree to which we will grow into the character of Jesus.

CHALLENGE

Take a moment right now and write down every negative thought you rehearse over and over that is trying to condemn you or keep you bound. After you take a minute to write down those negative words, you will be amazed at how bringing them into the light wins half the battle. Now, find a replacement for those words in the Bible and declare the truth over yourself. Read over them until those truths transform your mind. Let's pray.

PRAYER

Dear Holy Spirit, I ask You to bring to my remembrance every negative lie so that You can replace those lies with truth. I choose to come out of agreement with those lies and I ask You to fill my heart and mind with the truth that will set me free. I choose from this day forward to allow Your Word to renew my mind so that I can live in the freedom that You purchased for me. In Jesus' name, amen.

CHAPTER 8

The Proof Is in the Pudding

The proof is in the pudding is an expression that means the value, quality, or truth of something must be judged based on direct experience or results. The expression is an alteration of an older saying that clarifies the meaning: The proof of the pudding is in the eating. Once you have tasted something, you can then decide whether it is good or not. Scripture says, "Taste and see that the Lord is good; blessed is the one who takes refuge in him" (Psalm 34:8).

Let's look at some real-life stories of people I love dearly. I have walked alongside them, and they have overcome strongholds as they walked out their salvation and allowed the process of sanctification to take place in their lives. Don't just take my word for it. See how each one of these men and women of God broke free from the shackles of their own strongholds by applying what is written in this book. If they can do it with the help of the Divine Counselor, then so can you.

BREAKING THE STRONGHOLD OF DEPRESSION

HENRY SEELEY

I would never have identified myself as a person who struggled with depression. I'm not sure whether it was because I had been indoctrinated with the ideology that you couldn't be a follower of Jesus and struggle with depression, or because I was terrified to even open that door mentally. Looking back, it was probably a combination of both.

I'm genuinely thankful that I was raised in a faith-filled environment that taught us our first response should always be to take things to God. But somewhere in my early thirties, I found myself entering a dark season. I had been in full-time ministry for over a decade: leading worship, writing songs, producing albums, and touring the world. On top of that, my wife was also deeply involved in ministry, and we had two young children. Life was busier than ever.

The constant pressure to create, produce, and maintain the endless rhythm of church life was taking a heavy toll, and I was doing my very best to ignore it. The pressure wasn't just external. It was internal as well. The insatiable drive of a "creative perfectionist" was alive and well, though cleverly disguised under the pretense of "building the ministry."

On the outside, everything looked amazing! We were part of a thriving ministry that impacted lives around the world. "Creating for the kingdom"—what more could I ask for? But I wasn't prepared for the season when the doors of opportunity would begin to close and the constructs of my self-made, "all for the ministry" identity would start to crack.

As the months rolled on and the opportunities dwindled, I found myself striving harder and harder to prove my worth—to create, to produce, to validate my place in the ministry we had helped build. The harder I pushed, the darker things became internally.

The Enemy began to whisper lies. *You're done. You'll never write another song. Your best days are behind you.* I tried to push through, but it only made the heaviness worse.

I felt trapped. On one hand, I bore the immense responsibility to continue doing what I had always done. On the other, my sense of self-worth was being decimated. I felt worthless. Hopeless. Alone.

Sure, I had people around me, including an amazing wife. But I wasn't ready to admit my struggle, so I kept my walls up. After all, I was a minister—a worship leader producing music that was influencing countless lives across the earth. How could I have anything to complain about? I was exhausted physically and emotionally, spiraling deeper into despair. I was terrified that if I opened up, I would accelerate down the "road to insignificance."

Until one day I broke.

Utterly exhausted, through tears of despair, I mumbled words I never thought I'd say: "If I can't create, then there's no point in living. I feel like I'm going crazy, and I don't even know if I want to be here anymore."

It was a terrifying moment. The words felt like the cry of my soul I had been desperately trying to ignore. But it wasn't until I acknowledged the truth about what was happening deep inside that I could finally give God permission to start the healing.

One particular night, lying in bed, I felt a physical weight pressing down on me, as if trying to crush me into the floor. The more it pressed, the more I struggled to breathe. I knew it was spiritual oppression—a demonic attack—but I felt so overwhelmed that I struggled to even whisper the name of Jesus. My wife, aware of what was unfolding, began to war in prayer until the oppression lifted. It was in that moment that I knew things needed to change, and I knew it couldn't wait.

I canceled all my commitments. I immersed myself in worship, prayer, and God's Word. I began to deconstruct the layers that I had built up around me, my "ministry," my work, the bad habits and patterns that I had excused under the guise of "God's work," and I laid it all out before Him. The issue was twofold:

- My identity was not fully surrendered to Jesus.
- My heart didn't fully trust that God would take care of me.

I realized my value was rooted in what I did, not who I was—or more important, whose I was. I had been so caught up in *doing* that I had forgotten how to just *be*—to rest, to breathe deep, and to enjoy life with God.

Truthfully, almost any doctor would have diagnosed me with depression and anxiety, because that was the manifestation of what was happening in my life. But I knew what I was experiencing was deeper than the symptoms that plagued me, and I knew that whatever the doctor would prescribe—as helpful as it may have been in the short-term—would only mask the underlying issues that I needed to allow the Holy Spirit to address in my life.

And so began the journey to freedom.

Freedom is less a destination and more a pathway.

Freedom is less a destination and more a pathway—step-by-step, day by day, allowing the Holy Spirit to renew my mind and restore the broken places of my soul.

Over the following months, with the help of the Holy Spirit and some trusted, godly friends, I began to rebuild my foundations the right way—not depending on quick fixes but patiently allowing God to renew and transform me. It was hard at first—breaking down the familiar coping mechanisms that had become the crutches of my life. But the more I yielded to God, the stronger and healthier I became.

It's been nearly twenty years since that season. While there have been a handful of days when the Enemy has tried to pull me back into that darkness, I've stood firm on the Word of God, doing exactly as James 4:7 instructs: "Submit yourselves, then, to God. Resist the devil, and he will flee from you."

By His grace, I continue to walk daily in the light of that freedom.

BREAKING THE STRONGHOLD OF ANXIETY

ANDY RUSHING

> Do not be anxious about anything, but in every situation, by prayer and petition, with thanksgiving, present your requests to God. And the peace of God, which transcends all understanding, will guard your hearts and your minds in Christ Jesus. (Philippians 4:6–7)

On December 15, 2020, I came down with COVID-19. I had never been so sick in my life. From December 15 to January 4, I wrestled relentlessly with the disease but couldn't seem to overcome it. I ended up being sick for three weeks. During this time, I struggled with sleeplessness and anxiety about whether I would ever get better. I began to fear nighttime because I knew I needed rest to heal but also knew that I couldn't go to sleep.

One night I ended up going to the ER for what turned out to be a panic attack. I had never experienced anything like this before, but eventually I felt back to normal and was able to sweep it all under the rug since I was no longer sick. The sleeplessness and anxiety were gone, and I moved on with my life. What I didn't realize was that this had created a place in my heart where I didn't trust the Father. Because I never dealt with the root of it, I left a wound in my heart the Enemy could attack later.

Fast-forward a month. It was Friday, February 5, 2021, and we had just gotten our new puppy. As with any new puppy, he was struggling with sleeping through the night in his crate. On the second night, around 2:00 or 3:00 a.m., I was lying in bed after being woken up by him when, completely unexpectedly, it felt like a thousand-pound weight had been dropped on my chest. I felt alone, isolated, and like I was being pushed down into the bed, unable to move. The anxiety and fear had come back. All it took was two sleepless nights with a new dog to trigger the fear and anxiety I thought I had left in the past. This time, however, the Enemy doubled down and brought depression.

I had never been this anxious or depressed, so I knew this wasn't who I was, but I could not understand or figure out how it was consuming my life. Every waking moment was consumed by fear and anxiety, and then I would become depressed about feeling that way because I couldn't see any hope for an end. This cycle continued day in and day out. I would be at home with my family and feel a million miles away, or I would be in a room full of people and feel isolated, like there was a barrier I couldn't get through. I was under attack and could feel my life slipping away.

My flesh wanted to control the situation, because up to this point, I had never faced any adversity that I couldn't control myself. So I scheduled an appointment with my doctor to get help. My doctor prescribed medications that would help with anxiety and depression, but all they really did was treat the way I felt. All the intrusive thoughts and spiraling in my mind were still there; the medication just numbed the feelings. I honestly felt like a zombie, and I knew in my heart that the only way to truly fix this was the Lord.

At this point I had reached out to practically everyone for help. I had asked so many people to pray for me. I was vulnerable because I truly felt like I was at rock bottom. After almost a week of this, I was able to schedule a liberty session at the church. I wasn't sure what would happen, but I knew I needed freedom from this attack. I thought during the liberty session I would be prayed over and set free, but what happened was so much better than I could have expected and it became the catalyst to my freedom.

There wasn't this grandiose deliverance where all the anxiety and depression were cast off me. Instead, it was a still, soft moment of vulnerability where the Holy Spirit showed me the Father's love for me. I asked the Holy Spirit to show me how the Father sees me. What He showed me absolutely wrecked me: a picture of myself, innocent and clothed in white. I began to weep because in that moment, I knew I was fully clean. I experienced the full weight of God's love for me—His perfect love that casts out all fear. I had not been fully set free from the anxiety and depression yet, but I had a new understanding of God's love, and that became the foundation of my freedom.

I was still constantly being woken up in the middle of the night with anxiety and depression, and I began to fear the night and going to bed. I would lie in bed after being woken up, and all the *what-ifs* would run through my head. My mind would spiral. I would look at the clock and count down the hours until someone I knew was awake so I could call them to talk and ask for prayer. If I could talk to someone, maybe I wouldn't feel so isolated and alone. It was during this stretch of time that one afternoon Pastor Alex gave me a prophetic word: "This has only come on you, but is not in you, and this will be taken off you." I clung to this word because I knew it was from the Lord, and I knew He had given me hope for freedom.

A few days passed and yet again I was lying in bed—spiraling, feeling alone and anxious. I remember vividly the Holy Spirit speaking to me and saying, *Why are you lying in fear, waiting for someone to talk to? I am with you now, come and talk to Me.* I got up out of bed and went to my study, where I began praying and reading Scripture. He was true to His word; He was really there to be with me and talk to me.

The Holy Spirit began ministering to me, and I felt peace and comfort for the first time. He taught me how to pray over myself and my house. He showed me scriptures to pray at bedtime for peace and sleep (Numbers 6:26; Psalm 32:7; and Psalm 4:8). He even showed me how to truly worship, no matter how I felt inside. It was actually in the darkest, loneliest, most vulnerable, most anxious and depressed time that Holy Spirit was there for me with all the answers. I began developing a true intimate time with Him.

I had heard a message at the time that talked about shutting off the outside noise. I knew this was something I had to do. I had become consumed by my spiraling thoughts. As I was spending time in the Word, I felt prompted by the Holy Spirit to *turn off the outside noise.* So I simply asked Him, "Holy Spirit, would You turn off the outside noise?" In that moment, as real as if it were happening in front of me, He gave me a vision. I was sitting in a living room, representative of a peaceful place of comfort and safety. Sitting across from me was the figure of a man, but He was fully made of fire from head to toe. I instantly knew it was the Holy Spirit. He stood up and walked over to what was the "front door" of the room. As I saw this door, I could hear all kinds of noise coming through it, but I couldn't distinguish any of it. In a moment, He shut the door, and the noise instantly stopped. He simply walked back to His chair and sat down, as if to continue talking to me.

It was in this moment that all my intrusive thoughts, spiraling, and the *what-ifs* completely left my mind. The Holy Spirit had turned off the noise, and my mind was now a space only for Him and me. This was a pivotal moment. It marked the first tangible miracle on my journey to freedom.

Over the next week I began to sleep better and longer, sleeping through the night as the intrusive thoughts disappeared. The only thing I struggled with was wondering if they would ever come back. I'll never forget coming home from work one afternoon and asking Jesus if they would ever return. As plain as day, in my garage, Jesus gave me a vision of Him putting me in a vehicle and driving me away from the fear, anxiety, and depression. The farther He drove, the less I could see them until there was no sign of them left. At that point, He spoke to me and said, *Son, from what I have delivered you, will not return. I have set you free. This will never come back to you.* I began to weep in relief and joy.

At that time, I was still taking the medication from the doctor. There was still this element of me that felt I needed to be in control of something. I had felt the Holy Spirit prompt me to do a three-day water fast to reset my body and renew my mind in Christ. The day before I started, I had the thought, *Can I still take my medication while fasting?* Instantly, the Holy Spirit said to me, *Why are you putting a Band-Aid on something I am trying to heal? Get rid of the medicine and trust Me for your healing.* In that moment, I knew I hadn't fully surrendered my healing to Him. By continuing to take the medicine, I was agreeing with the spirit of fear, anxiety, and depression. I knew I had to surrender for my full healing. So without question, I gathered all the medication I had been taking and disposed of each and every one. As soon as they were gone, every last bit of fear, anxiety, and depression left me. Every doubt of permanent freedom was gone, and I knew I was free and healed forever.

From the moment I disposed of the medications until now, and for every moment beyond now, I am free and have been set free. There has not been an ounce of fear, anxiety, or depression on me again. It truly has been cast off me and will never return, and I live in full peace and confidence of this. I have not taken a single ounce of medication again, and I sleep through every night with peace and tranquility.

Disclaimer: This is Andy's experience, and not a substitute for professional medical advice. If you are currently on medication, please seek the advice of your medical professional before making any decision to cease medication.

It was actually on this journey that God showed me I didn't need to seek others for my healing. He is able to fully set me free in my home, in my secret place, just by seeking Him and surrendering. His love never fails. His love is perfect. It truly casts out all fear and is perfect peace. He loves me completely, and I love Him. Loving Him is obeying Him, and if for nothing else, this journey was such a blessing to me because it restored me to obedience to the Father. It reintroduced me to His love, mercy, and grace. How can I fear anything when I know and truly understand the Father's love for me?

BREAKING THE STRONGHOLD OF ANGER AND ADDICTION

NEIMAN DAVIS

> I lift up my eyes to the mountains—
> where does my help come from?
>
> (Psalm 121:1)

I grew up in the church with a family in full-time ministry. As a fourth-generation ministry kid, there was never an option not to go to church. In fact, even at a young age, I knew two things would be a part of my life forever: ministry and music. I was what I like to call a "back-door Christian," but not necessarily how you might think. The back door for me was through a green room. While I learned the importance of going to church, I focused more on how others would perceive me rather than learning that my identity should be rooted in Christ.

At the age of seven, I gave my life to Jesus. That same year, I was also introduced to pornography, which began to form thought patterns that as I got older would lead to unhealthy relationships and actions. Around this same time, I was diagnosed with ADHD and prescribed Adderall. When a doctor or a parent gives you a pill to take, you don't think twice about it as a kid. However, it quickly became the first substance I was addicted to; I would be hooked on it for over a decade.

At twelve years old, I had a traumatic moment in my life when I was molested. While I loved God and knew He loved me, I went into self-preservation rather than confession. Due to my family's ministerial status, I was afraid of bringing shame on them. Rather than talking about it, I kept it hidden. I often say that the loudest emotion is suppressed emotion, and that quite literally was the case for me for the next decade.

What started as toxic relationships with sex and pornography in my early teens led to trying other things. However, I never lost my faith. I knew God was real, and I saw Him work in other people's lives, but I always thought, *Can He do that for me?* I always felt a little too far gone. The idea that a big God could call me a friend was something hard for me to grasp. It was just easier for me to be "one foot in and one foot out" when it came to my relationship with God. I had experiences in His presence I couldn't deny, and prophetic words spoken over me that I believed to be true, but to sell out and give everything up for Him was opting for a boring lifestyle, in my mind. And being the fun-seeking enthusiast that I am, Adderall, psychedelics, and a myriad other substances seemed more appealing than being a "sold-out" Christian. I knew God, and I knew I was called. But I thought I could truly say yes to God and His plan for my life in the future once I was older and more settled.

In my early twenties, everything I had experienced and struggled with came to a head. I went into the darkest season of my life. Drinking and drugs became an everyday occurrence. During this phase, I had a hard time being around my family, and I just wanted to escape everything. I wanted nothing to do with ministry. All I wanted to do was play drums, tour, and make records.

One evening my entire family gathered at my grandfather's church to honor him for fifty years of pastoring. What was meant to be a celebration turned into a night when I almost lost my life. I overdosed and found myself in a hospital with a blood alcohol level of .348. I woke up after being unconscious for five hours and realized that something in my life had to change. Soon after that night, I got connected with a godly, Spirit-filled counselor who was also a pastor at the time. He began to work with me to identify the root issues in my life.

There were many times after my counseling sessions when I would try to get in touch with him, but he would not respond or get back to me for a week. I didn't realize it at the time, but he was putting healthy boundaries in place that were teaching me to work things out with the Holy Spirit on my own. I can also remember specific sessions with my counselor when the Holy Spirit showed up in an undeniable way.

One session in particular, my counselor and I were working through the anger I felt. As we were processing, I became increasingly more frustrated and irritable. Through discernment, my counselor informed me that what I was experiencing was an attack from a demonic spirit. As soon as he said that, the lights went out in the entire building. I immediately began to weep and was delivered. It was the first time I cried tears of tenderness and not of anger. I truly felt the wraparound presence of God in that moment. I went home that day and got rid of every drug I had.

As the intensive sessions came to an end, my counselor would give me assignments to act on that all involved prayer. I began to learn how to fill myself up with the Holy Spirit after a root had been dug up. Sometimes I had to choose to forgive someone, and sometimes I had to simply listen to my Father's voice. The last assignment he gave me was probably the toughest but also the sweetest.

The Enemy had tried to drive a wedge of distortion between me and my family for years. I was challenged to go to my parents' home and wash their feet without telling them in advance. The only parameters my counselor gave me was that if they tried to tell me no, I should simply tell them that I must do this. It ended up being the most tangible picture of restoration in real time that I had ever seen. Joel 2:25 says that God will restore the years the locust has eaten. He restores the lost years. After washing their feet, I was to leave their house and go pray for one hour. Looking back on it now, he was showing me how to take back territory that the Enemy thought he had. It was an event I will never forget.

In the early days of counseling and learning to hear the voice of the Holy Spirit, I began creating nonnegotiables in my life—truths about God and His nature that were unshakable, despite circumstances. I began to seek out promises in His Word and quite literally stand on them. Although I experienced radical deliverance in my life, I faced crippling anxiety in the years to follow that tried to overtake me. I remember being in the fetal position in my kitchen, crying and pleading with God to take the anxiety away from me. It took some time. It didn't leave immediately. But this is where those nonnegotiables became a reality for me.

> Since then, you have been raised with Christ, set your hearts on things above, where Christ is, seated at the right hand of God. Set your minds on the things above, not on earthly things. (Colossians 3:1–2)

The practice of daily proclaiming Scripture and prayer helped me get to a place where, when anxiety would rear its ugly head, it would not overtake me. I've learned to recognize the thoughts and fears that are not of the Lord and combat them with the truth of Scripture. Isaiah 26:3 says, "You will keep him in perfect peace, whose mind is stayed on You, because he trusts in You" (NKJV).

Through my journey of counseling and learning to hear the voice of the Holy Spirit, I had to deconstruct the parameters (lies) I had put around my faith and reconstruct them through the lens of how Christ had seen me all along. In that process, God was with me every step of the way, and I quickly found out that I was not alone.

If you feel alone, know that the Lord is speaking to you. Take it from me. I've been there. Know that it gets better. It takes one step of turning toward Him. Instead of putting all your thoughts and energy into what you currently see, look up to Jesus.

I needed help, but it took me deciding to lift my eyes above the situation and see that help was available. He's there for you every minute, every hour. Just call on Him. I promise He will change your life. He surely has changed mine. I have a healthy, restored relationship with my family; an incredible wife and daughter; and I am walking out the call of ministry I felt as a kid all those years ago. If He can do it for me, He can do it for anyone.

BREAKING THE STRONGHOLD OF FEAR AND SHAME

JOSH SILVERBERG

> Do not be afraid; you will not be put to shame.
> Do not fear disgrace; you will not be humiliated.
> You will forget the shame of your youth.
> (Isaiah 54:4)

In 2014, I found myself in a dark place—isolated, depressed, addicted, and consumed by the relentless demands of the music industry. I had lost my sense of direction and felt like I was constantly chasing something I could never attain. I was operating from a place of fear and lack, failing to realize that I had already "made it." My value was in what I could achieve, instead of in what Christ has already perfectly performed. Thankfully, Stacey Willbur, a trusted friend in the music industry, mentioned that she was attending a church called The Belonging. Her words struck me, and I felt an undeniable pull to go.

The strong message of identity that was preached at The Belonging ignited a personal revival within me. I made a decision: I was going to believe that every single word of Jesus was true and start living like it—even if I didn't feel it yet. This transformation led me to confront demonic strongholds and lies that had been afflicting me without me even realizing it.

One of these strongholds manifested as extreme fear and panic during flights. I would worship, pray, read my Bible, and do everything I could to calm myself, but nothing worked. Intense fear and anxiety would take over—my heart would race, my body would shake, and I couldn't stop the overwhelming thought that

I was going to die. That was when I noticed a disconnect between my life experience and the words of Jesus.

I found myself asking, *Why do I feel like a hostage to fear when Jesus came to set the captives free?* I didn't feel free at all. But because I had decided to believe Jesus' words as truth, I knew I had to keep pressing into prayer until I was living in that reality. Praying for myself wasn't enough, so I reached out to my pastors, Alex and Henry Seeley, for prayer. By that point, I had built a relationship with them over the years, serving at church and witnessing incredible miracles of God on the prayer team.

On the very day I was scheduled to meet with them, I woke up from a dream that shook me. In the dream, I was on an airplane, and there was only one seat left—all the way in the back. I sat down next to two people whose heads and faces were distorted. They started joking about the plane crashing. One of them said, "Do you smell that? That must be fuel. We're definitely going to crash." They laughed as if it were amusing.

As I sat there, feeling smothered by them, I looked down at my wrists and noticed tattoos that read: "Jesus Saves." Then I woke up.

That evening, I arrived at my pastors' house and met with them in their basement. It was a day I will never forget. I told them I wanted prayer because I didn't believe I should be afraid or panicked, especially on airplanes. With compassion in her eyes, Alex asked, "Are you okay if we ask the Holy Spirit to reveal the source of this fear?"

I agreed, and we prayed. Then Alex asked, "Are you getting anything?" I hesitated before responding. *Yes . . . but I don't see how it's related.* When we prayed, a buried memory surfaced—one I had not expected.

I was reminded of a time when I was sexually abused—raped—as a young boy. It was something I had never spoken about, not to anyone, except my wife, Michaela, just that week. Looking back, I believe it was the Lord prompting me to share and preparing me for this prayer time. Alex responded, "Let's come out of agreement with fear and shame."

She asked me to repeat after her: "I come out of agreement with shame."

Before I could even get all the words out, I shook violently and let out a high-pitched scream.

It felt like something had left me—something that had been with me for a long time but was never truly *me*. The demonic power that had held me hostage was gone. The lie I had believed—rooted in shame and fear—was broken.

I was set free.

Not only from uncontrollable panic on airplanes but from so much more. It felt like a fundamental shift in my personality. Insecurities and fears that I had previously accepted as part of *who I was* were now gone. Even a victim mindset that I hadn't realized I carried had been healed.

This freedom transformed my life, even in the music business. Before, I would read contracts and only see what was being *stolen* from me. Now, I could assess agreements logically, without being manipulated by emotions or fear. My deliverance from that day changed so many areas of my life—my career, my marriage—it could fill an entire book.

I thank the Lord that His words are true! He has come to set the captives free. I am forever grateful for Alex and Henry, for pastoring me so well and taking the time to pray for me that day. That is a day I will never forget.

BREAKING THE STRONGHOLD OF UNDEALT WITH CHILDHOOD TRAUMA

MORIAH CRUZ

> So do not fear, for I am with you; do not be dismayed, for I am your God. I will strengthen you and help you; I will uphold you with my righteous right hand. (Isaiah 41:10)

I grew up in a Christian Latino home. Jesus was always present in my life, and for as long as I can remember, He felt like a real friend. Some of my earliest memories include reaching to touch the wall and imagining Jesus reaching back to touch my hand, both of our hands meeting.

My home was filled with love, but I also remember the stress, fighting, and fear. My parents faced financial struggles raising three kids, and their fights involved yelling and explosive anger. I lived with constant fear of upsetting them or seeing my siblings get into trouble. My parents came from childhoods marked by abandonment and poverty. They worked hard to get an education and relocate somewhere safe to offer a better life for their children. Despite their work ethic and determination, they lacked communication skills, boundaries, and an understanding of how to discipline in love.

As a child, I understood their intentions. Now as an adult, I see the depth of harm they caused and their human limitations. My parents were tired and stressed. They often worked late, and we didn't always know when our next meals would come. Our house was never clean. Our feet were black from walking barefoot in the house and at times, we came home from school to find the electricity cut off.

I was the firstborn. I learned early that being quiet and well behaved made my parents grateful. Not being a burden was a way I could contribute. Unbeknownst to me, I formed core beliefs that shaped my life:

1. Being small makes me easier to love.
2. My parents have big problems and having my own needs or desires will overwhelm them.

Parents are a child's first concept of God and these beliefs about my parents translated into the beliefs I had about God. God was busy managing real issues like wars and global injustices. He seemed angry and exhausted. It was best if I didn't bother Him. I didn't know then that He noticed or liked me, that He remembered everything I did. I didn't know He saw me when I was lonely or nervous on my first day of work. He was always with me. He would meet me in the middle of the deepest pain and longings I didn't know existed. But I didn't know any of this yet.

At age nine, I became curious about death. What would happen afterward? Is it scary? Curiosity is normal for kids, but mine turned into a longing. I believed that life would be easier for my family and even God if I wasn't there. I kept this thought to myself, secretly testing the strength of curtain rods and blinds, searching for a successful way to hang myself. Eventually, I found comfort and relief in cutting with paper clips and pens before moving on to box cutters. I cut my legs to keep it hidden. The burn and sting felt like releasing air from a high-pressure ballon ready to burst.

Between seventeen and nineteen, my mental health spiraled out of control. I began having severe panic attacks that left me very disoriented. I experienced spontaneous crying episodes, which I now recognize as flashbacks of sexual abuse. These flashbacks seemed to originate from a very young age and a memory I couldn't recall. This left me foggy, confused, and terrified. I thought I was going insane. I began failing assignments and tests. I was afraid that my mind would drive me to kill myself and I felt powerless to stop it. I felt unsafe as if someone took over my thoughts. I tried to self-medicate with unprescribed pills, but things became worse. I grew paranoid that my boyfriend wanted to kill me and I began to hear voices. I wasn't sleeping or eating. I quit my job and felt sure I was going to die. I took my father's gun and slept with it under my pillow until I wasn't afraid to die anymore. I chose a date where I could die in the woods.

But before that day came, someone invited me to a weekend retreat at church. I thought it would either help me or I would die anyway. I arrived and met eyes with an event worker. She stood calmly, loving, and smiling. I heard a clear, kind, gentle, and authoritative voice say, "I've been waiting for you." I knew it was Jesus.

If God spoke to me, I had expected him to tell me how disgusting I was and to repent. But I experienced warm love and gentleness. That night, at church, I felt God's presence. I could not stop physically trembling and shaking. I walked in afraid to be seen by God, but instead I felt Him see me to protect me. That night, I slept in the room they prepared and for the first time ever, my mind was completely quiet. The internal scream completely stopped. I slept like I hadn't slept in years.

The next day was filled with teaching and worship. We were

invited to receive the Holy Spirit and I knew this was for me. I went up for prayer and felt like I was completely blasted by a pressure washer with warm love, joy, and light. I felt darkness and torment leave. I could not stop smiling and laughing. I had never felt so alive. I couldn't stop thanking God.

I asked Him the best way to thank him. Should I sing, jump, or stay on my knees? His response shocked me. I clearly heard him say, "I want you to eat." I hadn't eaten in about four days, and food was the last thing on my mind. I was free to eat! It seems small, but this was one of the kindest, most unforgettable moments. I had never felt so happy to enjoy a meal. I felt like Jesus was making lunch and I was overwhelmed with joy.

That weekend changed everything. I began a deep relationship with Holy Spirit and God's Word. His presence was everywhere. I felt His kindness when I woke up, His peace and care when I ate, and His nearness when I prayed in the spirit on my way to work. Scripture became manna to me. I couldn't get enough. I renewed my mind daily with Romans, Psalms, and Deuteronomy. My heart burned with gratitude as I read the Gospels, and the Holy Spirit began giving me dreams and words to encourage others. That was almost twenty years ago, and it was the start of a journey toward becoming whole.

Six years later, I married an incredible man. Five years into our marriage, I decided to pursue counseling for the first time. I was looking for help with my episodic rage, sexual dysfunction, and a deep-seated fear of returning to school. After months of therapy, I finally shared about my flashbacks with my husband. Days later, I wasn't sure what to expect but to my surprise, he admitted he had been unhappy in our marriage since the beginning.

I went from seeking therapy to grow and heal to suddenly facing real marriage trouble. The cruel beliefs I carried in childhood resurfaced: be small, be easy to love. I felt shattered and completely unprepared. It exposed the childhood trauma I didn't know I still carried. Still, we were committed to making our marriage work. We sought counseling, which helped mediate conversations, helped me see from his perspective and apologize for the ways I contributed to hurting our marriage. With counseling, church mentors, deeper relationships, and serving, our marriage was beginning to shift.

I began going on walks with Jesus where He invited me to let Him be my Counselor and tell Him everything, no matter how small. When deeper wounds surfaced, I told Him every fear, hurt, worry and disappointment. In turn, God told me His thoughts toward me. He convicted and corrected me, showed me the ways I idolized or held on to pride, and always left me feeling blown away by how seen, loved, and forgiven I was by Him. He used our walks to heal the lies that had shaped my whole life.

But just as things were getting better, COVID 19 hit. As a nurse, I had just transitioned from cardiac ICU to ICU float pool. This meant that I would exclusively work COVID ICU for the year. I had never in my career witnessed so much death. I spent hours on the phone with grieving families. I felt helpless. Sleeping and eating became difficult. Drinking became a way to unwind but soon became a means to feel normal. It broke open yet another layer that needed healing. Life became unmanageable. By the end of the year, I was more than fifty pounds underweight.

I decided to step away from patient care and enter residential treatment for six weeks. Even when I couldn't feel Him, I never felt God abandon me. I invited Him into my therapy sessions. His truth and His Word became my foundation as I processed not just the grief of the pandemic, but the deeper layers of grief within my marriage and my past. We addressed my insecurities and fears, revisited my flashbacks, and I was given tools to pull myself out of emotional and mental loops.

I am grateful for therapy. It was invaluable in my growth as a friend, nurse, and spouse. Skilled professionals helped me address root causes, identify mental health conditions, and receive safe, effective treatment. Medication greatly alleviated my symptoms of anxiety and depression.

But only God truly found me in the depths. Only He pulled me from the ocean of despair. He never once forsook me. The Holy Spirit revealed His love, a love that transcends everything I am and everything I am not. He saw my efforts, my fears, my unspoken hopes. He saw me whole—past, present, and future.

Looking back, I can see Holy Spirit's hand in every healing moment. At the retreat, He delivered me from darkness and restored my mind. In marriage, He revealed the deep wounds of my past. He carried me through the trauma of COVID and taught me how to rebuild.

Healing wasn't a single moment. It was a journey that took time and the steady presence of God. It took renewing my mind, returning to His Word, and letting the Holy Spirit show me who I really was. Because of God, I am courageous. I am unshakable. I dream again. I see a future filled with hope, love, and expectation. I am happy to be alive because I now understand my purpose, and I am so grateful for the power of Jesus Christ who has healed and delivered me.

THERE IS NO JUNIOR HOLY SPIRIT

> People were also bringing babies to Jesus for him to place his hands on them. When the disciples saw this, they rebuked them. But Jesus called the children to him and said, "Let the little children come to me, and do not hinder them, for the kingdom of God belongs to such as these. Truly I tell you, anyone who will not receive the kingdom of God like a little child will never enter it." (Luke 18:15–17)

Children are the most receptive and faith-filled humans on the planet. They take adults at their word, and many believe anything they are told. Before we opened our kids ministry at The Belonging Co, I had one request for our leaders, and it was this: The children are not to be treated like babies. This will not be a childcare facility. Rather, it will be an extension of what happens in the adult service because the Holy Spirit reveals Himself regardless of age. There is no junior Holy Spirit! It is imperative for our children to understand the peace and person of Holy Spirit so they have the tools to navigate life with Him. I experienced Him at a very young age and understood the power of His love and forgiveness, and so will the children in our kids ministry.

Henry and I have carried this same perspective as we've raised our two children. Since they were young, I prayed that our children would overcome issues at an early age that often take adults years to overcome. I believed they didn't have to learn only through therapy and education, but that Holy Spirit would be their Divine Counselor as they continued to grow. Here are some more testimonies of the power of Holy Spirit. You'll see anxiety exchanged for peace and fear exchanged for perfect love in my own children's lives.

BREAKING THE STRONGHOLD OF THE FEAR OF DEATH

TAYLOR SEELEY

It was the spring of 2016, and my son, Taylor, who was nine years old at the time, was so excited because my husband had nailed a wooden ladder into the large tree in our backyard. He loved climbing trees and enjoying the outdoors. One day when I was away traveling and speaking, and my husband was downstairs in his studio working, Taylor decided to go out and climb his favorite tree. He had climbed to the top of the branches, about twelve feet high, when suddenly his foot slipped. He fell out of the tree upside down and landed on his head. He said later that he felt like he went unconscious for a few moments after his fall. He stumbled into the kitchen, and when he got inside, he started groaning because he couldn't speak or cry out for help.

Henry heard a strange sound from upstairs and recognized that it was Taylor's voice. He knew immediately that something was wrong. He ran upstairs to see what had happened, and to his shock, there was Taylor, his face bruised and bloody, and his mouth covered in dirt. He couldn't put a sentence together. He just kept asking, "Where's Mommy? Where's Mommy?" Henry did not know what had happened, but he quickly realized that Taylor must have fallen out of the tree.

Henry instinctively placed him in the back of the car and raced to the hospital. During the entire ride, Taylor was not making sense, so Henry kept praying in the Spirit. All Taylor could repeat was, "Where is Mom? Where is Mom?" Henry kept saying, "Mommy's traveling, bud. She's not here right now," but Taylor would forget immediately and repeat the same question even after Henry had just answered it. Henry had to overcome the immediate fear and dread that came over him and begin to declare in faith that God would take care of Taylor.

They arrived at the ER. As the doctor was checking him from head to toe, they were astounded that Taylor hadn't broken any bones or experienced greater damage, considering how far he fell and the way he landed. By the end of the examination, the doctors said Taylor was totally fine. His mind returned to normal; he retained information spoken to him, and could clearly articulate back. He even asked Henry for ice cream, and that request told Henry that Taylor was fine.

We thought it was over and everything was okay. He had a few scratches on his face, but what happened next we did not expect. He began to develop an irrational fear, which resulted in panic attacks. At first, they were few and far between. We just thought he was going through a stage, and it would work itself out. The following summer, we went overseas, and over the course of two weeks, we encountered four major tragedies. While we were in Leeds, UK, there was a shooting at a concert, and someone died. We left Leeds and traveled to London. The day we arrived, there was a stabbing on the London Bridge. Then we went to Paris, and there was a shooting on the steps of Notre-Dame. On the way back to London, we stayed in Notting Hill, and the night we arrived, the Grenfell Tower burned down. Many people died in that fire. We were staying one block away from the tragedy, and everywhere we went—every café, storefront, and streetlamp post—had pictures of young kids who had been declared missing.

As Taylor witnessed these images, it triggered a panic attack, and we had to go back to where we were staying because he was overcome by the spirit of fear. When we returned home to the States, the panic attacks became more frequent and very severe. He was so afraid of forgetting to breathe and of dying that he would have trouble breathing. Because of this irrational fear, he became overwhelmed and could not calm down. We had to teach him to breathe in and breathe out until he felt safe and could regulate himself again.

I was overcome with worry for Taylor and began to pray for this fear to break off his life. As I prayed, I asked Holy Spirit to help me lead him into freedom. I remember hearing the still, small voice of Holy Spirit saying, *You need to get to the root of where this fear was established and have him come out of agreement with it.* I went to him at a time when it was safe and quiet, and I explained the process of asking Holy Spirit to set him free. I led him through the same inner-healing Sozo method that I mentioned earlier in the book.

I asked Taylor to close his eyes and imagine Jesus next to him. I asked him to repeat after me and invite Jesus to come and be near him. He closed his eyes, invited Jesus, and immediately saw a picture in his mind's eye of Jesus sitting next to him. He said he felt safe with Jesus there. I then asked Taylor to repeat this prayer after me: "Lord Jesus, I invite You to come and show me when this fear came into my life." He sat quietly with his eyes closed for a moment. He then said, "Jesus said the fear started when I fell out of the tree and got scared." I then asked him to pray this prayer after me: "I let go of the spirit of fear and give You those feelings. I ask You, Jesus, to shine Your light on the lie that locks in this fear." I asked him to ask Jesus what lie he had believed that caused him to feel scared. He immediately answered, "I fear I am going to die young."

My heart was so heavy as I watched my beautiful son, who had been carrying a fear of death without knowing how to heal from it. My eyes welled up with tears, and I asked him to pray this prayer to Jesus: "Please replace the lie with Your truth." He sat there for a moment and said, "Mom, Jesus told me He has my life in His hands, and He will protect me. He will not hurt me, and I need to trust Him with my life." Well, I just about fell over because I was watching in real time the power of Holy Spirit ministering to his little heart.

He began to cry and thank Jesus for making him safe and for saving his life. We ended our time thanking Jesus and Holy Spirit for revealing truth. I prayed a prayer that went something like this: "I break the power of lies and the spirit of fear over Taylor. In the name of Jesus, cover him with the blood of Jesus so it won't come back again. I ask You to fill Taylor with Your peace and truth. Amen." We hugged and cried, and I waited to see what would happen in the coming days. My son is going to be eighteen years old this year and he has not had a panic attack since that day. God heals what is revealed at the source.

When we see, hear, or experience something traumatic or frightening, fear can enter our hearts. Lies from the Enemy are like a fortress that imprisons us and keeps us locked in the fear that we've come into agreement with. When these lies keep us from doing normal things like sleeping in the dark or breathing, as Taylor feared, then we become prisoners to that issue. The Bible is clear when it says, "God has not given us a spirit of fear, but of power and of love and of a sound mind" (2 Timothy 1:7 NKJV). God's truth is a light that shines on the dark areas of our souls and breaks open that which keeps us bound.

> "If you hold to my teaching, you are really my disciples. Then you will know the truth, and the truth will set you free."
>
> (John 8:31–32)

> I sought the LORD, and he answered me;
> he delivered me from all my fears.
>
> (Psalm 34:4)

BREAKING THE STRONGHOLD OF NIGHT TERRORS

HOLLY SEELEY

> There is no fear in love; instead, perfect love drives out fear.
>
> (1 John 4:18 CSB)

We had lived in the United States for two years and Holly was eleven years old. She made some great friends, was enjoying school, and was growing more familiar with our new city. That year, she gave her heart to Jesus and was filled supernaturally with Holy Spirit. During that winter, she went to a school friend's house where they often played. One day, I picked her up from her friend's home, and she told me that she had a great time. We rode home together and she updated me on what was going on at school—a normal mother-daughter chat in the car. We got home and had dinner like every other night. When it was bedtime, we tucked our kids into bed, said good night, and turned out the lights.

I went downstairs, my husband started the fireplace, and we sat together enjoying our evening in the living room. Around 11:00 p.m., I remember vividly staring at the fire, pondering things that were happening in my own life, when I heard a bloodcurdling scream come from the upstairs bedrooms. I immediately ran upstairs to see what had happened. Holly was in a dreamlike state, screaming out, "No, Slenderman! Go away. No, Slenderman. Go away!" In between her screams, she woke up, ran into my arms, and began to cry. I asked her what was going on. With tears running down her cheeks and her little body shaking, she began to tell me about a horrific nightmare she had. I carried her downstairs so we wouldn't wake her brother, Taylor, and as we sat by the fire, she told me that, in her dream, Slenderman was trying to kill her.

I asked, "Who is Slenderman?" She told me that earlier that day, while she was at her friend's house, the older sister had been on her laptop watching this evil show called *Slenderman*. Holly had caught a glimpse of him on the screen and heard him talking, which immediately made her feel uneasy. Even though it was only a few moments of seeing something she shouldn't have, it was enough to terrify her. I had never seen Holly full of terror like I did this night. I felt the Holy Spirit prompt me to pray with her and have her come out of agreement with that moment before it could take root as a spirit of fear in her life.

So, I did what I knew to do. I asked her to close her eyes, and I presented Jesus to her so that she could see Him in her mind's eye and allow Him to do some kingdom business in her heart. Once she had closed her eyes, I asked where she saw Jesus in that moment. She answered, "Jesus is on a bench at the park." I asked her where Slenderman was in her mind, and she immediately said, "He is sitting right next to Jesus on the bench." I asked how she felt in this picture, and she replied, "I feel safe because Jesus is here." I then asked, "What does Jesus want to do with Slenderman?" I remember thinking, *Oh, I cannot wait to hear what she says next! I'm sure she is going to say that Jesus killed him, and he was destroyed.* But something profound came out of her mouth. With her eyes still closed, she said, "Jesus is hugging Slenderman, and the more He hugs him, the more Slenderman is dissolving into nothing." She said that Jesus hugged him so much that he disappeared and then Jesus came over to her and held her in His arms.

She began to cry. She said she felt that all fear had left her in that moment. I was stunned. That is not what I was expecting, but when I asked Holy Spirit what to say in response, He reminded me of the scripture, "There is no fear in love. But perfect love drives out fear, because fear has to do with punishment. The one who fears is not made perfect in love" (1 John 4:18). This was incredible. I could not have made this up if I tried. I looked in her eyes and said, "That is right, Holly. Jesus dissolved that fear by showing you that it is perfect love that drives it away. Jesus is not afraid of Slenderman, but what He was wanting you to see is that when His love shows up, nothing can be evil or fearful in His presence."

From that night on, all fear left her heart and her dreams. She never had another nightmare about it again. Holy Spirit reveals the truth of God's Word to bring healing and deliverance in the moment. I declared over Holly that she would not be consumed by a spirit of fear because that spirit does not come from the Lord. God gives us power, love, and a sound mind (2 Timothy 1:7).

When we allow the revelation that perfect love from the Father is what actually changes us, then transformation can truly begin. It means we get to experience a profound shift in our understanding of God's love for us and how it affects our lives. This revelation signifies that we are no longer bound by fear, which causes us to self-protect and live with coping mechanisms. When we receive this, we are able to live from a place of validation and trust that Father, Son, and Holy Spirit love us more than we can ever imagine. When we live from the security of this place, we live with confidence in who we are and a greater sense of peace and purpose to do what God prepared in advance for us to do.

I don't know about you, but after reading these testimonies, my faith is stirred. If God can do this for them, He will do it for you. I hope these real-life stories have encouraged you to seek the same Spirit that delivered them to help deliver you. We all have access to the supernatural power of the Holy Spirit to change us, if we allow Him to lead us. When we cooperate with Him and *do* the work required, He will be faithful to completely heal us. If we take the time to call on Him, He will answer and gently show us the way through our pain that will lead to complete freedom. Our role in all this is to listen and obey. I can promise that you will have freedom on the other side of your obedience.

Right now, you can ask Holy Spirit what those strongholds are in your own life. Maybe they have already been highlighted as you have been reading this book, but you have the choice: to remain in agreement with the lie or come out of agreement with the lie that you have been believing. Are you ready to be free? If so, let's pray and declare this prayer over your life.

PRAYER

Jesus, I praise You for who You are. You are mighty and victorious over all my enemies. Your eyes have seen the injustice that I have suffered as I have believed the lies that have held me captive. I ask for Your forgiveness for my agreeing with the Enemy's lies that have built a stronghold in my mind and caused me to operate in the flesh. I utterly renounce and reject my sin and ask You, Jesus, to forgive me, cleanse me, and teach me Your ways. I lay aside every fear that ties me to the past. I let go of all bitterness from unjust treatment against me. I forgive those who have hurt me and release them from my judgment. I now tear down every stronghold in my mind and soul and I choose to believe Your truth about me and my circumstances. I command my mind and emotions to come into kingdom order whereby I will be led by Holy Spirit and not by my feelings and ungodly thoughts. I give over complete control of my life and surrender my rights to You, Jesus. I now destroy every assignment from the Enemy that has tried to steal, kill, and destroy my life. I dethrone the spirit of fear, and any other spirit that has had control over me by choosing to follow Jesus and to obey the voice of Holy Spirit. I now boldly declare the truth of Your Word: "If the Son sets you free, you will be free indeed" [John 8:36]. In Your name, amen.

CHAPTER 9

Learning to Know His Voice

One of the most common questions I get asked is, "How do I know when it's God's voice speaking to me?" Many people get confused and wonder, *Is this God speaking, or are these just my thoughts?* My friend Debbie once led a session on how to hear God's voice and asked everyone this question: "Has anyone ever heard a voice in their head that said, *You are an idiot*? or *You are useless, you can't do that*, or *You are weak*?" She read out an entire list of negative words, and by the end of her question, all of us had our hands raised. She said clearly, "Well then, you can hear the Enemy's voice loud and clear. So why would God allow the Enemy's voice to be clearer than His when He longs to be in relationship with you?"

We all agree that the negative chatter in our minds is not from God. So, if we're able to tune in to negative words, then we should be able to stop and listen to the words of affirmation and instruction that come from Holy Spirit. He speaks into our thoughts, and if you hear a condemning word or an accusatory word, you can know immediately it is not God because the voice of God never contradicts the Word of God. He cannot lie and will not condemn or make you feel ashamed. He is kind. He is good. And even when He brings correction, He will never cause you to question your identity or the way He sees you.

> "My sheep listen to my voice; I know them, and they follow me. I give them eternal life, and they shall never perish; no one will snatch them out of my hand. My Father, who has given them to me, is greater than all; no one can snatch them out of my Father's hand. I and the Father are one." (John 10:27–30)

> "To him the gatekeeper opens. The sheep hear his voice, and he calls his own sheep by name and leads them out. When he has brought out all his own, he goes before them, and the sheep follow him, for they know his voice. A stranger they will not follow, but they will flee from him, for they do not know the voice of strangers." (John 10:3–5 ESV)

When we live fully immersed in Christ, we position ourselves to constantly hear from Him. I think we have overcomplicated hearing God's voice—I believe it's easier than we think. As you continue to meditate on the Word and fill your heart and mind with God's voice, you'll begin to pay closer attention to the thoughts that enter in. You'll learn to quickly discern whether they are from His Spirit or from the Enemy. Once you have learned what His voice sounds like, you will be tuned to hear His voice, and you will grow in confidence over time.

For example, I can be in a crowded room with hundreds of people talking at the same time, but when either one of my children or my husband calls out my name, I immediately turn to find them because I am familiar with the sound and tone of their voices. The reason I can recognize their voices anywhere is because I have spent decades living under the same roof and communicating with them daily. They are not strangers; they are family. I know their voices, and they know mine.

God's voice becomes so familiar that we almost mistake it for our own thoughts. That is how supernatural our lives should be when we are walking in faith and being led by the Spirit. This is why we can sometimes miss the voice of God—we dismiss it as our thoughts. God's voice is often gentle, so we need to be near enough to hear Him. Here are some practical keys to hearing God's voice.

ENGAGE WITH THE SCRIPTURES

> All Scripture is inspired [God-breathed] by God and beneficial for teaching, for rebuke, for correction, for training in righteousness; so that the man or woman of God may be fully capable, equipped for every good work. (2 Timothy 3:16–17 NASB)

One of the clearest ways to recognize the Holy Spirit's voice is through Scripture because His voice sounds like the Word of God. Jesus was the Word made flesh. He has fidelity with His Word, because He is the Word. John 1:1 says, "In the beginning was the Word, and the Word was with God, and the Word was God." Scripture is how you learn His tone, character, and truth.

That means when the Holy Spirit speaks, it will always align with Scripture. If all Scripture is God-breathed, then it's not meant to be quickly read. It's meant to be ingested. We have to feast on the Scriptures and allow it to read us because these words are alive, active, useful for teaching, and able to correct our thinking.

When the Holy Spirit speaks, it will always align with Scripture.

Ingesting and engaging with Scripture means meditating on it and applying it to every part of our lives. We cannot use it to suit our narrative. I have met believers who want what they want and twist Scripture to fit their desires instead of coming with an open heart to receive God's truth. We either believe the entire canon of Scripture is the final authority, or we don't. We cannot pick and choose the parts we like and discard the parts we don't like when it comes to reading and obeying God's Word. Many have memorized verses, but the disconnect happens when Scripture is merely head knowledge and does not lead to heart transformation.

When I sit down to read the Scriptures, they should encourage me but also rebuke and correct me. If we only want the warm, fuzzy feeling that God loves us, then we rob ourselves of Holy Spirit being our teacher. We must read the Bible and allow it to permeate our being. His voice, through the Word, leads us into truth. And the more we engage with it, the more we begin to recognize when it's Him speaking.

We must let the Word dwell in us so it can change us from the inside out. Colossians 3:16 says, "Let the word of Christ dwell in you richly" (ESV). When we need instruction in an area, Holy Spirit brings to our remembrance the Word of God we need for that particular situation. But if there is no Word dwelling inside us, we cannot draw from the library of God's Word to lead us.

I say this all the time to our church: We must not just be

hearers of the Word but also doers of the Word. The Word is like a mirror. When we look into it, we immediately see who we are supposed to truly look like. But when we turn away from the Word and focus on how the world lives and continue to live with worldly mindsets that don't align with Scripture, we forget the truth and fall into the trap of what *seems* good in our own eyes (James 1:22–24). Holy Spirit speaks to our hearts through the Scriptures so we can carry His words with us wherever we go.

> "This is the covenant I will make with them
> after that time, says the Lord.
> I will put my laws in their hearts,
> and I will write them on their minds."
> (Hebrews 10:16)

CHECK THE MOTIVES OF YOUR HEART

> The heart is deceitful above all things
> and beyond cure.
> Who can understand it?
>
> "I the LORD search the heart
> and examine the mind,
> to reward each person according to their conduct
> according to what their deeds deserve."
> (Jeremiah 17:9–10)

We all hear through a filter, and if that filter is dirty, wounded, or cluttered, it will affect our hearing and how we live. Many of us come to God in prayer and just talk the whole time, telling God what *we* are doing. In essence, we are leading the conversation the entire way and we're not positioning ourselves to hear. Then we become confused and wonder why we have suddenly found ourselves in a mess. When things go wrong, we turn around and blame God, but He didn't do anything wrong. We led the way, took control, and then asked *Him* to follow *our* lead instead of praying and listening for His direction through His still, small voice within our inner man. The more we allow the Holy Spirit to clear away the noise and clean our filter, the more clearly we'll be able to hear Him.

In my season of rebellion, when I wanted to stay with my boyfriend who I knew was not right for me, I felt the small whisper of Holy Spirit say, *No. This isn't the man for you.* But I wanted to be with him, nonetheless. I vividly remember sitting across from this boy who was asking me to be his girlfriend, and I heard the very voice of God impress upon my heart that this would not go well for me. But I chose to ignore that still, small voice because I wanted to be with him.

I carried a deep spirit of rejection that convinced me I was unworthy of being loved. So when the first boy showed interest, regardless of whether I liked him or not, I clung to him. I decided he was going to be mine so I could feel loved, even if it was in a broken way. For the next three years, we were on and off in our relationship. I made awful decisions that hurt him that led to much pain and regret. I ended up falling in love with him because I gave so much of myself to him. Our soul ties ran so deep that it took me four years to release all the ties I had made with him.

Then when I finally broke up with him out of obedience to the Lord, I became mad at God because He was not changing my heart or desire for him. All the while, I knew God had a calling on my life, but I hadn't dealt with the rejection in my heart. I disobeyed and then expected God to do all the work for me. However, it was up to me to repent, turn away, and follow Jesus. Every time I wanted to go back, I had to *choose* to do the right thing, and Holy Spirit gave me the strength and grace to live righteously.

If you're reading this right now and Holy Spirit is bringing a relationship to your mind that you know is not from Him, or He's revealing an opportunity that you know you need to say no to, listen at the first prompting. Check your heart and ask Holy Spirit, "Why is it so hard for me to let go? What motives in my heart are unchecked or unhealed?" Reflect on whether your actions are driven by genuine care for others or whether self-interest, fear, or pride might be influencing your decisions. Ask God to reveal the hidden hurts of your heart and bring healing as you surrender to Him. And then obey His voice. Obedience is what God is after, and when we obey, we live blessed lives according to Scripture. The more we learn to hear and respond to His voice, the more confident we become in recognizing it. And over time, obedience won't feel like loss—it will feel like freedom.

TAKE TIME TO BE STILL AND LISTEN

Could it be that we are not tuning in to the voice of Holy Spirit because we are not staying still and quiet long enough to hear His voice? Could it be that with all the noise going on around us, we are looking for a dramatic manifestation of His power but are not willing to wait for the Word of the Lord to come to us? This is

Stillness trains your spirit to tune in.

why Joshua encouraged the people of God to meditate on the Word of God day and night. Stillness trains your spirit to tune in. It's not just silence. It's making space for intimacy.

Elijah fled after a threat was made against him by Queen Jezebel (1 Kings 19). He left his servant behind and ran far away in fear for his life. During this time, God led him to a cave on the mountain of Horeb, the place that represents intimacy with God. As Elijah poured out his heart in self-pity and fear, the Lord told him to stand on the mountain in the presence of the Lord because He was about to pass by and reveal Himself to Elijah.

Scripture goes on to say that there was a great and powerful earthquake, but God was not in the earthquake. Then there was a great wind that swept by, yet God was not in the wind. After that came fire, but the Lord was not in the fire. And after the fire came a gentle whisper. When Elijah heard it, he pulled his cloak over his face, went out, and stood at the mouth of the cave. Then the voice said, "What are you doing here?" It was in the gentle whisper that God's voice was revealed. To hear a whisper, one must be close to that voice.

The word *whisper* in Hebrew is *demamah,* which can be translated as "silence" or "still."[1] Take some time and be still. Wait on the Lord to speak as you open your mind and heart to hear His words of revelation for transformation. When I need to hear His voice, I will go into my bedroom and turn off all the noise and sit in my chair or bed, whichever feels right at the time. I close my eyes, and I ask Holy Spirit to speak into the situation that I am facing. I then wait in the silence, quiet my mind, and rest in knowing that He will answer me. I will sometimes receive a thought that I know is from Him because I would not have thought about it myself or because I don't want to do what He has just asked because it means humbling myself and doing what is right. But every time I listen and obey, He brings me into peace that surpasses all natural understanding.

You can practice learning to hear the voice of Holy Spirit every day. When I was learning to listen to Him, I would practice with little things. In fact, I still do this! My family laughs at me, but it works every time! When I have lost something in the house (and let's face it, this is becoming a regular thing as I get older), I sit still for a moment and ask Holy Spirit where I last placed the item. I'll say, "Please show me where it is," and I kid you not, every time, a thought will drop into my mind. I go directly to that place, and the item is there!

I know it may seem silly, but this is how you can develop sensitivity to hearing the voice of the Spirit guiding you. If Holy Spirit takes the time to help you with the everyday things, how much more does He want to speak to you about emotional and spiritual things that will bear lasting fruit? This is how a relationship with Holy Spirit grows.

JOURNAL WITH THE LORD

Journaling is another great discipline to develop as you practice hearing God's voice. It helps you process, discern, and revisit what He's said. There is something liberating about getting things off your chest and giving them to the Lord in a safe space. When you are writing your vulnerable thoughts down on paper, you are essentially pouring your heart out to the mother heart of

God and He longs for you to share with Him openly even if it is on paper. Your words can flow freely as you make your thoughts known on pages that you can go back to over and over. God hears our prayers, and sometimes the most profound therapy for us is to write down our heart's cry and watch God do a miracle over time.

So use a journal to write down what you hear, and get in the habit of recording the thoughts and impressions God gives you so you can look back over the words He has spoken. I remember reading Romans and coming across the verse that says "What, then, shall we say in response to these things?" (8:31). I stopped and thought, *What are the things He is showing us?* As I reread the previous verses, I began to journal all the things that were accessible to us as we learn to walk by the Spirit of God. I came out with a list of twenty things God has given to us because of Christ's resurrection power. As I read them out loud, my faith increased because Scripture was showing me how to live my life according to the power of the Spirit. I encourage you to read Romans 8 for yourself and see what God reveals to you personally.

The words throughout the Scriptures will encourage you and give you that second wind when you feel stuck, or you feel like God is not speaking. I have often gone back over old journals and read entries from months or years past that ignite faith in my heart. Sometimes, God asked me to do something that I have yet to obey, and when I read over His words again, it brings those instructions back to my remembrance. I can then act upon the last thing He told me to do.

Journaling also helps keep a record of the answered prayers in our lives, which increases our faith to move forward. It allows us to be honest and see how far we have come over different seasons. We can look back and see that God's hand was moving—even when we felt He was silent.

SEEK GODLY COUNSEL

> Where there is no counsel, the people fall;
> but in the multitude of counselors there is safety.
> (Proverbs 11:14 NKJV)

One of the ways Holy Spirit helps us recognize His voice is through others. Sometimes He speaks through godly counsel—people who help confirm what He's saying, challenge our thinking, or point us back to truth when our emotions cloud our judgment. As I've said in previous chapters, counselors have their place in our lives for a season, but when it comes to learning to hear God's voice clearly, finding the right counselor matters.

If you are seeking a counselor, make sure you find someone who understands the power of God at work in our lives. They must understand that God is the One who heals, and He alone holds all the power. Human counsel has been so helpful to me over the years through pastoral care. Counselors have helped me identify the root of where pain began, but they have always led me to Jesus, the One who healed the brokenness and changed my life. Counselors can give language for the things we struggle to make sense of, and they can also send you home equipped to apply the truths that come from Scripture to your everyday life. Look for people who have fruit in their own lives and in the lives of those they have counseled rather than someone who simply keeps you on a merry-go-round, rehashing your issues, but never gives you the tools or truths for lasting freedom.

Mental health resources are meant to equip you with tools to live well and help you navigate making the right choices, not keep you dependent. It breaks my heart that there may be people in this industry who have no interest in seeing people get free but instead may exploit their clients. I am not saying all counselors or therapists operate this way. It is important, however, to recognize this reality. This is why you need to choose wisely who you open that door to.

There are those who truly want to see you free from your issues, and then there are others who will be a coping mechanism for the rest of your life, offering comfort but never leading you to real healing. With them, freedom feels like a wishful hope, rather than a possible reality. The right counsel won't speak over Holy Spirit. They'll help you recognize when it's Him speaking, and encourage you to follow where He leads.

BE IN COMMUNITY

> And let us consider how we may spur one another on toward love and good deeds, not giving up meeting together, as some are in the habit of doing, but encouraging one another—and all the more as you see the Day approaching. (Hebrews 10:24–25)

The Holy Spirit doesn't just speak in private. He speaks to us through the people within our community. He uses people to confirm, sharpen, and stretch us. Learning to hear His voice sometimes means listening to the people He uses to speak on His behalf. I often get asked by people, "Why church? Can't I just have a relationship with Jesus? Do I *have* to be involved in a church? I like Jesus but I don't really like the church."

Friend, please hear me. The church is how God designed the body of Christ to function. It was His idea and His plan for all of us to engage in spiritual formation within the context of community. God never designed us to be alone. He places the lonely in families, and He Himself is in community with the triune God: Father, Son, and Holy Spirit. It is within community that "iron sharpens iron, and one man sharpens another" (Proverbs 27:17 ESV). What does that mean? A piece of iron cannot get sharp on its own. It needs another piece of iron to create the friction that sharpens the blade.

> The Holy Spirit doesn't just speak in private. He speaks to us through the people within our community.

Though church community will never be perfect, it should be healthy. And when we place ourselves in a Spirit-led community, people can come alongside us and help us stay sensitive to God's voice. They keep us accountable from going astray, call out the blind spots we can no longer see in ourselves, and when life is difficult, there is nothing sweeter than having your community come around you in solidarity and encourage you through a tough season.

The Lord often brings prophetic words or words of knowledge through people who speak life into our present and our future. These moments give us hope, but most important, they reflect our covenant-keeping God who promises He will never leave us nor forsake us. The church becomes the hands and feet of Jesus as we yield ourselves to Holy Spirit's leading and love for one another. Spiritual growth, sanctification, instruction, and accountability happen in the church in a way it cannot outside of it.

My assistant of five years came to us as a broken, fragile person. She loved God and had made Him her Savior, but there were many areas where she was still bound to her past. I watched as the power of Jesus through Holy Spirit set her free, but it happened in the context of community. Here is her story. I hope it encourages those of you who are afraid of allowing yourselves to be vulnerable and open to a community of believers.

FREEDOM FOUND IN JESUS AND THE CHURCH

SAM EUDALEY

For as long as I can remember, I navigated the world in a self-imposed armor of hyperindependence. A childhood home filled with sexual abuse, physical abuse, emotional abuse, and the chaos of addiction taught me that relying on anyone was a risk I could not afford. When I was fourteen, I went to live with my grandparents. My grandfather, a man of quiet strength and unparalleled kindness, made the first crack in my armor. He was the first person I noticed who wore a cross necklace, which felt strangely significant, a silent pull toward something I could not name.

Nearly a decade later, I finally understood the pull I'd felt. It started with a simple error: a mistaken concert date that led me to a Tuesday night at The Belonging Co, and a life-altering encounter with Christ. I gave my life to Christ and my journey into Scripture began. I would hear messages painting a portrait of God's character: His relentless pursuit after us, His unconditional love, and His gentleness. I would wrestle each time, but in His unwavering kindness, the Holy Spirit met me—every time, in every doubt. Except one.

> The LORD is my rock, my fortress and my deliverer;
> my God is my rock, in whom I take refuge,
> my shield and the horn of my salvation, my stronghold.
> (Psalm 18:2)

I remember wondering, after years of healing and finally embracing God as a loving Father, did I really need to see Him as a protector? A defender?

It felt like my hyperindependence was something I could not surrender. It was my self-constructed sanctuary. Yet, this sanctuary began to crumble when I started struggling with my mental health. I turned to counseling in search of answers. Counseling gave me the language to understand I was experiencing involuntary PTSD flashbacks and disassociating. My mind and body were reliving traumatic moments and to them, it was as if they were being plunged right back into the raw, unfiltered reality of those moments with brutal immediacy.

One night, after a flashback, I was lying on my bedroom floor with worship music washing over me. The words of a song I held close in this season, "He never told me that it would be easy. He said suffering would come, but He promised peace,"[2] resonated with a newfound truth. It was in my weakness, in my surrender of my hyperindependence, that I began to glimpse the possibility of His protection. I realized that true healing was not about my ability to control but about trusting God's promise of peace even during chaos.

One year at our church conference, God gave me a vision during worship of an operating room. I was on the table, and there was the surgeon and his team around him. When someone undergoes surgery, you generally get to choose your surgeon, but you do not get to choose your surgeon's team. I felt like God was reminding me that He's the ultimate surgeon, the ultimate Healer, but we get to choose the team around us to help us along the journey. That team can include church community, co-workers, friends, family, and therapists. But it's a reminder that the intentionality of who we choose to surround ourselves with, especially in the valley, should point us to the ultimate Healer.

We were designed for community, not isolation. I have learned that real strength isn't about doing it all alone. Instead, it is a gradual surrender to the vulnerability of trusting Him, releasing control into His capable hands, relying on His power rather than mine, and trusting His unwavering presence in our lives as the ultimate Healer.

CHALLENGE

I love Sam's story. It's such a powerful reminder that God created us for communion with Himself and with others. As you reflect on everything we've explored in this chapter, I want to encourage you because I believe Holy Spirit wants to speak to you even now.

Before we go on, why don't you get yourself to a quiet place, settle into a comfy chair, and practice tuning in to your ability to hear Holy Spirit? In this process, first prioritize prayer. Ask Him to speak and be in a posture to listen. Before you read God's Word, ask Holy Spirit to illuminate something in the Scriptures, and practice journaling. Cultivate a quiet heart and open yourself to hear whatever God says to you. Learn to spend time engaging with and meditating on Scripture. Make a habit of expressing your thoughts and feelings through writing, as this can help you discern the Spirit's guidance. You will be amazed at what starts to flow out of you! And allow others to hear what God has been speaking to you.

At first, it may seem like your thoughts, but as you align with God's Word and His thoughts, you will begin to naturally hear His beautiful, still, quiet voice impressed on your heart. And as you continue to do this, I promise this will become a natural practice in your everyday life. Just as many of my friends—whose testimonies you've read—waited to hear the voice of Holy Spirit and experienced freedom in their souls and clarity in their minds, the same can happen for you. Enjoy!

CHAPTER 10

Living a Spirit-Led Life

A few days before our annual church conference, I was sitting at my desk preparing the message I was going to preach that week. Immediately after I sat down to write, I felt this horrible sensation in my chest. It felt like heartburn at first, but it was so overwhelmingly painful, and I'd never experienced anything like it before. I once heard that after a certain age, a sudden chest sensation that comes from nowhere and feels like heartburn could be the onset of a heart attack. I'm not normally a person who jumps to the worst-case scenario, but I remember going downstairs and saying to my husband, "I think I need to go to the ER."

One thing you need to know about me is that I don't go to the ER unless I really believe something is wrong. I went to the ER, and they immediately did an EKG. Praise God the tests came out clear, and it wasn't a heart attack. At that point, they suspected that I might have a stomach ulcer. They sent me home with a prescription for an antacid and told me to come back if it got worse. I remember thinking, *Oh, I don't really believe I have a stomach ulcer. I'm a pretty healthy person, and I don't suffer from stress or have a very acidic diet.* But I went home and hoped for the best.

As the evening progressed, I was in agony. I'd never felt such pain in my chest, and it was excruciating. I did not sleep at all that night. I tossed and turned as the pain increased. The hospital had given me the contact information for a gastroenterologist and instructed me to make an appointment the next morning. My husband knew something was very wrong as he watched me writhing in pain, so he called the specialist. She said she couldn't see me until the following day, but if I started vomiting blood, Henry should take me back to the ER. No more than five minutes went by after that conversation before I began vomiting blood. I couldn't believe it. Henry put me in the car, raced me to the ER, and had to drop me off at the door because it was during 2020 when the COVID-19 restrictions were at an all-time high. He reluctantly left me there as I stood alone with a bucket of blood.

The nurses immediately scrambled to get me into a room. They pumped me with morphine, the doctor came and immediately scheduled an endoscopy, and to my utter amazement, they found a mass in my stomach. They were not able to get a biopsy that day because their equipment couldn't reach deep enough into my stomach, but they confirmed it was definitely a mass and said they would need to take a closer look. I remember being so frightened. I was all by myself. I wasn't allowed to have visitors that entire week due to the COVID-19 pandemic and I was on morphine, with very few answers to what was happening inside my body.

I lay there on that hospital bed with so many unanswered questions. I was completely alone with my thoughts, with nothing else to distract me or pass the time. I didn't even have my Bible with me. As we rushed out of the house that morning, I took only the clothes on my back, which were my pajamas. I had no overnight bag—nothing. I sat in the hospital by myself for four days, completely alone, and yet I was at perfect peace. I honestly never *felt* alone. I never felt fear come over me. I was reminded of the scripture that says, "You will keep him in perfect peace, whose mind is stayed on You, because he trusts in You" (Isaiah 26:3 NKJV). When we are faced with a difficult situation like this, we have two options: to trust God and know that He has us covered or freak out entirely and allow anxiety to overwhelm us.

Any area of your life that is under paralyzing anxiety ultimately reveals that you are struggling to *trust* God. The root of all anxiety is fear. We need to ask ourselves the question, What is it that we are most afraid of? This is where Holy Spirit helps to reveal the root of our fear. Is it fear of being abandoned? Fear of being alone? Fear of loss or betrayal? Fear of death? Whatever it is, we must ask Holy Spirit where the fear originated and ask Him to heal the core wound. Trust me, this is so important. I have done this several times over the course of my life, and it is why I can be in the middle of chaos and hardship, and be still and know that He is God. This is the goal for every believer: to know their God and not be tossed by the waves of adversity.

This is something you will have to become familiar with for the rest of your life. I have been walking with the Lord for forty years and I have had to make a decision to choose peace and trust God every time, no matter how dire the situation is. We either worry ourselves sick and nothing changes, or we choose to place our trust in the One who is greater than all. Faith is a muscle that needs to be exercised consistently, and as you practice it over time, you become strong. Life won't stop giving you hardships, but the quicker you are at learning how to exercise the fruit of the Spirit of peace, the sooner you will live in that supernatural peace.

It's uncanny how you can be in the middle of the storm and know that you are going to be okay because you have developed a life of intimacy with Holy Spirit, which leads you to trust Jesus with your life. It was at that moment I said to the Lord as I was lying in that hospital bed, "I feel like I have passed a test—the test of trust. I trust You with my life, and therefore, I know that You will carry me through this. I am not alone, and You are my healer." I sensed Holy Spirit say to me, *This is a spirit of affliction that has come upon you. It will not lead to death, and you will show others how to walk through a season of uncertainty with faith. You will show people how to depend on Me.*

I walked through that season of being diagnosed with stomach cancer for four months at the age of forty-seven, and I had never felt so near and present with the Lord, who led me daily into His presence. Because I had been spending years in His presence, I was able to be in perfect peace. It wasn't a peace that made any sense in the natural, but a peace that could only come from Holy Spirit. He led me through the scriptures I had memorized. The Word of God became my guide. I chose to follow the leading of Holy Spirit.

The Bible says to "be anxious for nothing, but in everything by prayer and supplication, with thanksgiving, let your requests be made known to God; and the peace of God, which surpasses all understanding, will guard your hearts and minds through Christ Jesus" (Philippians 4:6–7 NKJV). Even when I was fully convinced the tumor had disappeared and the CT scan showed it was still there, I took that to Jesus and declared in faith that I was healed. God encouraged me with the story of Hannah in the Bible. I chose not to sit and wallow, but instead "stand up" and petition God again in prayer for my miracle. In December 2020,

I went back to the hospital for my third scan, and to the doctor's amazement, the tumor had totally disappeared. I had been healed supernaturally.

I think the most powerful part of this testimony wasn't the healing or the disappearance of the tumor. It was the deep peace I had, no matter the outcome. We all long for peace. It's one of the deepest desires of the human heart. I believe that's why so many people turn to drugs and addictions, because those things allow them to escape to a place that feels calm and detached from the trauma they are facing. But we have peace in a person, and He manifests Himself through the fruit of the Spirit in our lives. It's what the world is craving, and it is what we have living inside us. When our lives are full of peace, the world takes notice. Ultimately, that is why we need to understand that the peace that surpasses all understanding guards our hearts and minds in Christ Jesus (Philippians 4:7). These are not just pretty words on a page. These words are the living, active Word teaching us how to function when all hell breaks loose over our lives. This is how we put the Word of God into practice. If we want to have peace, purpose, live life abundantly, and stay free, we have to be led.

> If we want to have peace, purpose, live life abundantly, and stay free, we have to be led.

Our Christian walk should reveal the goodness of God in our lives, no matter what we go through and no matter what the outcome is. I believe this is how God's glory gets revealed—when we look different from the world and go through trials and trauma but come out on the other side without being destroyed. Our purpose in life is to bring God glory and that happens when we live our lives set apart from the world and reveal that God is good even when life does not go as planned.

> For we are God's handiwork, created in Christ Jesus to do good works, which God prepared in advance for us to do. (Ephesians 2:10)

God did not put us on this earth simply to exist. According to Scripture, we were created on purpose for a purpose. We were created in Christ to do good works, which God prepared in advance for us to do. This means that before you were knit together in your mother's womb, the Lord already knew and called you by name. You were never an afterthought to Him. He has specific, tailor-made plans that He wants to carry out through you. But the Enemy, knowing our God-given potential, will attempt to do everything he can to thwart those plans. He will sow seeds of doubt, despair, and even death.

This is why people are tempted by suicidal thoughts, especially when they feel as though they've lost all hope and have no real purpose left. When your purpose is gone, your will to live begins to diminish. Life was never just meant to be about us. Accumulating more and more material things, chasing happiness, and focusing on self ultimately leave us void and empty. It's only when we walk in the purpose given to us by the One who created us that we will have a reason to wake up every morning and experience true and lasting fulfillment. But we can't do that on our own. We must be led by God in every area of our lives in order to live life with peace and purpose.

Life is about being fully present, sharing what you uniquely carry, and leaving an indelible mark on the world. If you have a reason to be alive and you know why you were placed on this earth, then you'll have the will to live. It doesn't mean life is perfect or that you are never sad or never have a bad day. But if you know why God placed you on this earth, you'll feel alive because you understand your purpose. I truly believe purpose is the most important thing that we need to grasp. When you lack purpose in your life, you lack the clarity needed to see why you were placed here and what it is that you uniquely bring to the world around you. That doubt, when left unaddressed, takes root within you and makes your life feel hopeless. Many people struggle with purpose anxiety, the negative emotional state, including stress, worry, and frustration, that rises in us from struggling to find meaning.

Sometimes as we walk through life, it can feel aimless or even overwhelming, especially when we face countless choices, feel the pressure to reach perfection, and are surrounded by so many voices telling us what we should do.

At times, walking out our lives as Christ followers can feel like climbing Mount Everest. Life is not easy and it's not a linear path. It often feels like an upward climb with obstacles and dangerous terrain to navigate before we can reach the summit. When we seek Him first, His kingdom, and His righteousness, He really does add all the things in life that we need. We find true rest for our souls, and we discover who we are and what we are meant to do.

But in order for that to become a reality in our lives, the key is to follow His teaching and His leading. Jesus was our greatest example of being a follower. Yes, I said follower, because even though He was fully God, He was also fully man and completely submitted to following only what the Father told Him to do. He never did anything apart from the Father's instruction. Before and after every time He ministered, He went to the Father in prayer. He was completely dependent on Father and Holy Spirit while He was here on earth. He lived a perfect life. If Jesus needed to be fully dependent on the Father and Spirit, how much more should we be? He showed us the way forward through the Scriptures, and if we intend to live a life that reaches the summit of peace and fruitfulness, it will only be because we are led by the Spirit.

When researching about Mount Everest, I learned that having a climbing sherpa is essential if you want to stay alive and reach the summit, especially if you are a novice climber. A sherpa is a personal guide who is local to the area and has a deep understanding of the mountain. Their profound knowledge of the mountain enables them to guide anyone and take them on the path that leads to an awe-inspiring encounter, not death. Many sherpas work as guides, but they also do the dangerous work of setting up the ropes and ladders that climbers use to make their way to the summit. They climb beside the mountaineer and are a source of good advice, bringing their experience of going up the mountain. They set up base camp and help carry the load, provide food, and transport the oxygen tanks and medical supplies as they navigate the course ahead. It is not recommended to climb Everest without a sherpa.

Of course, some people think they can do it all on their own and at a pace that will break records. But one of the greatest problems they encounter is that many of these mountaineers lack sufficient experience and training. They are overly ambitious about reaching the top of the mountain. They underestimate how difficult it can be and become a little too confident for their experience. Some see that there are only eight hundred meters left to the summit, and in their minds, they have already finished. They decide the last section will be a breeze. But in their lack of wisdom, they stop listening to the guide. This is when the climb becomes extremely dangerous. Some mountaineers become so obsessed by their own egos that they ignore the safety warnings of their sherpas and press on to the summit without them. Many have died because they ignored the leading of the sherpa.

The same can be said of us when we walk this journey of faith without relying and depending on God's leading. We can become too familiar and think we are just fine on our own. We let go of the leading of Holy Spirit because we have somehow deceived ourselves into thinking we're safe, we're good, and we don't need Him anymore. Basically, we say, "I'll take it from here," and then find ourselves in trouble because we took our pride and arrogance with us along the journey up the mountain, fully convinced we could climb it on our own.

When Jesus approached His disciples, He said to them, "Come, follow me" (Matthew 4:19). He didn't ask them to lead; He asked them to follow. The disciples had access to Jesus 24/7 for over three years. They watched Him perform miracles, heal the sick, and preach the gospel. They could ask Him anything at any time. He was teaching and guiding them to live on earth with a kingdom mindset, and all they needed to do was follow His lead. So why would we ever want to ignore His leading in our own lives?

When we become born-again believers, Holy Spirit takes up residence within us. From that moment, a constant battle begins between our flesh and our spirit man. The word *spirit* refers to Holy Spirit, who dwells in every believer. Our walk is our daily relationship with God. Our flesh refers to our carnal nature, which is predominantly selfish. We must choose to be led by the Spirit rather than by our flesh. The ongoing work of sanctification happens when we submit our will and emotions to the leading of Holy Spirit so we can live a flourishing life. We are always being conformed to the likeness of Jesus, but if we think this just happens by osmosis, we are in for frustration and disappointment.

We must learn to listen to Holy Spirit's voice, obey His prompting, and allow Him to lead us into all truth. What does that mean exactly? Being led is about surrendering your right to be in control and placing your trust in the One who knows better—in this case Holy Spirit, who is God—even when it doesn't make much sense or feel great. The word *led* is a verb, indicating that our surrender to the Spirit's leading is an ongoing act of our will, a choice we must continually make.

There have been so many times in my life when I have had to learn the hard way. I am quite stubborn by nature and have had to learn to submit my will to God in the areas of my life where I may not like what the Holy Spirit is leading me to do. My flesh wants to take control and reason with the Lord, offering explanations for why I shouldn't have to go through with what He is asking me to do. But this has never led to His peace or fruit in in my life.

I remember when God asked me to shift the gatherings we were having in our basement from once every two weeks to every week. I sensed the Lord asking me to go all in with the group He had entrusted us to lead in that season. My flesh did not want to because I knew it meant more work for me. I was preparing a message twice a month and now He was asking me to study and pray for a word for the group every single week. I did not want to give up my comfortable life when I was not really working. I had been in the United States for over a year and had become a little too familiar with not having to go to church every Sunday morning or exert myself in serving others. I knew where this was leading, and I did not want to go there.

I wrestled. I reasoned. I made every excuse—until one night, it was as if the Lord took over my mouth as I was in a worship moment in our basement. The Spirit of God was moving profoundly in people's lives, and I was overcome by His presence. I have always been in awe of what He does when you just allow Him to move. At the end of the meeting, I said, "Well, I love this so much that I think it's about time we did this every week." As soon as the words left my mouth, I felt a wave of anxiety come over me. I had just said something out loud that I was now going to be held accountable for by the one hundred people who were in that basement. It was stretching, and it was not a great feeling. Yet as I yielded my will to His and obeyed His voice, I saw God move in exponentially greater ways than I had ever seen. More people were being impacted and discipled, while simultaneously God was enlarging and strengthening my capacity. My ability to minister grew in consistency, and we were seeing more miracles and fruit from being obedient.

More than anything, God had a plan for The Belonging Co to be birthed in Nashville, Tennessee. And if I had resisted that prompting, perhaps we would still be in our basement with only 120 people. God knew He wanted a church like ours in this city. All I needed to do was yield to His plan and follow His lead. I'm so thankful He led us to this place because thousands of people have been impacted for His glory because we chose to follow and obey. Submitting your flesh to the lordship of Christ doesn't always feel good, and it requires you to push through. But when you get to the other side, it is so worth it! I wouldn't be able to do what I do today if I had stayed comfortable and committed to what felt easy at a pivotal moment when God was asking me to step out in faith.

Jesus was led by the Holy Spirit into the wilderness for forty days and forty nights to be tempted by the devil. Scripture doesn't say He wanted to do this. You simply read that as soon as He was baptized, "Jesus, *full of the Holy Spirit,* left the Jordan and was *led by the Spirit* into the wilderness, where for forty days *he was tempted by the devil*" (Luke 4:1–2, emphasis mine). There was no negotiation, no discussion—just a yielding to and obeying the Spirit's leading.

The wilderness was not a place of punishment but rather a time for Jesus to overcome the Enemy. This empowered Him with authority to minister. If He had forfeited that season, He would not have shown the Enemy and the powers of darkness that He had authority to overcome temptation. God tests all of us, just as He tested Jesus—not to make us fail but to strengthen us. In the wilderness, Jesus gained dominion over the Enemy and made right what Adam and Eve made wrong in the garden of Eden through their failure and disobedience to God the Father.

I love how Darrell Johnson explained this, saying, "The word translated 'temptation' is the Greek word *peirasmos*, which has two different meanings. One is 'test'; the other is 'temptation.' A test is something meant to prove a person's character and, in the process, improve it. A temptation is meant to entice a person to sin, to bring a person down in some way. Whether it is a test or a temptation depends on who is behind it and how we respond."[1]

God does not tempt us. Therefore, we know that it is the Enemy who tempts us to sin. But God will use tests to refine and grow us, and the prayer of our hearts should be the Lord's Prayer: "Lead us not into temptation but deliver us from evil" (Matthew 6:13 ESV). That means, "God, please don't allow the Enemy to turn my test in this situation into a temptation that will cause me to sin." This is why we must be led by the Spirit of God and always immersed in the Word of God so that when the Enemy does come to distract us, we have a stronger defense against him just as Jesus did in the wilderness. Jesus did not engage with the Enemy in conversation. He simply declared, "It is written," every time the devil tried to get Him to sin (Matthew 4:1–11). Satan couldn't win because Jesus allowed the Spirit of God to lead Him in all truth.

Sometimes we are led by the Spirit into uncomfortable seasons, but we must not mistake this as God punishing us. There are times when being led into a difficult season is for our benefit. The Lord is conditioning us to gain authority over the Enemy and our flesh. So much of what we walk through in the wilderness is a dying to self. This is required if we are ever going to apply what we have learned from Scripture and from Holy Spirit.

When we find it difficult to obey, we typically have a lordship issue because if Jesus is our Lord *and* Savior, then we don't have a right to say no to Him. Having a Lord means living in submission to His authority. The lordship of Christ means that Jesus is the ruler over us, and our posture is to obey because we can *trust* that He is always leading us to what will benefit and not harm us. I've noticed this problem within the church. Some

Christians love to view Jesus as their Savior, but not their Lord. People love the idea of Jesus saving them, but they don't always like having Him as Lord because this means they aren't in control of their lives. He is. Some Christians find it difficult to obey the Holy Spirit's voice because they have not completely surrendered to the lordship of Christ.

You can be one of two people: a church attender or a Christ follower. If you are just a church attender and not a Christ follower, you will constantly live with a divided heart. I think one of the main reasons people don't follow Him wholeheartedly is, first, because they do not know what the voice of Holy Spirit sounds like. This can be the result of a shallow relationship with Him and a lack of knowledge of God's Word. Second, many have allowed sin to remain active in their lives, creating spiritual blockages that make it difficult to hear Him clearly. We must decide to follow Jesus, no turning back and with no compromise. We can't claim Jesus hasn't fulfilled His promises if we haven't consistently given Him all we have over time and then witnessed the fruit of that obedience. Don't give up prematurely and assume that God is not who He says He is. Stay the course, follow His lead, and watch Him transform your life from the inside out as you yield to the Divine Counselor.

Jesus was obedient unto death. He did hard things. He listened and obeyed the Father's voice from the time of His baptism until His death. When Jesus was facing imminent death He said, "Father, if you are willing, take this cup from me; yet not my will, but yours be done" (Luke 22:42). I am sure Jesus didn't go to the cross jumping, leaping, and praising God and yet, He obeyed His Father's leading. He did what was difficult.

While Jesus was praying this prayer to His Father, He

experienced a physical manifestation of intense emotional and spiritual anguish. Scripture describes His sweat as "great drops of blood" (Luke 22:44 NKJV). This likely represents a medical condition called "hematidrosis," where blood is present in sweat.[2] This condition is rare and can be triggered by extreme stress or emotional trauma. This shows me that He was overwhelmed by what was being asked of Him, but He chose to go through it for our sake. It was, as the Bible says, "for the joy set before him he endured the cross" (Hebrews 12:2). It was hard, and yet He followed through.

He gave himself up for us and died a brutal death because He understood that on the other side of His obedience and surrender was the gift He would be able to give all of us. The punishment that He suffered brought us peace. He broke the curse of sin and death once and for all, so that we would no longer be bound to the Enemy's curse. He purchased our freedom so we could live as sons and daughters of God, reconciled back to our original design as God intended when He created us. We are now heirs with Christ!

Jesus wants us to live totally surrendered and fully submitted, just as He modeled for us, because it is the most fruitful life we could ever experience. It's only when we live in complete surrender that we feel the safest and most secure. Many of us get stuck when we find ourselves at a fork in the road, and do not know what direction to go or what decision to make. How can we

Jesus wants us to live totally surrendered and fully submitted, just as He modeled for us, because it is the most fruitful life we could ever experience.

know where God is leading? We can know where He is leading when we have fully surrendered our will and allowed Him to be the leader.

Our will is strong, and it is the only thing God won't change or force. When we are presented with the truth (the call to repent and be born again), God gives us the ability to believe. By His grace, we can be rescued from spiritual death and brought into new life. If we were not given the ability to choose and self-determine, love would be impossible, and so would the ability to reject evil. Our ability to choose operates within the framework of how God designed us and the world we live in. We must take responsibility and surrender our will. It is not a matter of whether you can, or you can't. It is a decision of whether you will, or you won't. It's that simple. We can say, "I can't forgive someone," or "I can't change," or "I just can't bring myself to do the work," but ultimately, we can choose to do anything we put our heart and mind to.

I understand life can be hard at times. Make no mistake, life is difficult for me at times, but I am an overcomer. I am living proof that Jesus' power lives inside me. Because He has already won the victory, I am able to fight the battles alongside Him as I meditate on His Word. I have to apply the Word day and night, commune with Him day and night, fill my life with His presence day and night, and listen and obey day and night. It is an ongoing process that gives me the supernatural ability not just to cope through life, but to flourish day and night.

We are all being led, by truth or by lies. So, now it's your turn to choose. First, choose to allow Holy Spirit to lead you into all truth, and do the work necessary for your healing. Then, you will be able to write your story and testify to others of what

Holy Spirit has done in your life. You've heard my stories and my friends' stories. You've heard Scripture, science, and truth. Will you decide, from this day forward, to make Holy Spirit your first option? The One you go to? The One you lean into? The One you obey? He wants to renew your mind, heal your soul, and reveal the purpose that has been prepared for you in advance to fulfill. The responsibility is yours. You cannot make excuses anymore. It's been laid out for you in the pages of this book.

You get to exercise your free will and decide whether you will be a doer of the Word or just a hearer. You can continue making all the excuses for why you can't be healed or free. You can blame everyone else for what happened to you, or you can take responsibility. You can cast your cares to the Lord for He cares for you. You can do the work that is necessary to build your spiritual muscle. And you can become a reflection of the glory of God here on earth and lead others into freedom as you yourself have found it in your life.

Don't allow the Enemy to steal one more day of your life. The Divine Counselor is waiting for you to invite Him into your life so that He can lead you to the One who died for you and rose again so you can live in resurrection power. We can do better when we know better, and I pray that this book has led you to the One who knows you better than you will ever know yourself.

CHALLENGE

I challenge you: Make the necessary changes that will lead you into the life you have always dreamed of. The call is free, and it's for everyone, including you. The process is costly, so make the decision to be all in, and I can promise you that the rewards will be priceless. For you to live your life according to your God-given purpose, you must lay the correct foundation. I pray that you will not just read the Word and put it back on the shelf, but that you will apply all that Holy Spirit has illuminated to you from His Word. I also pray that God takes you to places you never thought possible. Don't be afraid. Take the first step and allow the love of God to permeate your mind, body, soul, and spirit, and watch what He will do in and through you. I know you won't regret it. The time is now. You really can do it when you allow the Divine Counselor to guide you every step of the way. God bless you.

Acknowledgments

When writing a book, one may think that it is a solo project, but the reality is, it takes a village to make the finished product that you are now reading or listening to. And so I want to give honor where honor is due. I first want to thank my family, who understands that when I'm working on a manuscript, I am preoccupied for several months with writing. Thank you, Henry, Holly, and Taylor, for the way you support me and love me through every process of seeing my vision come to fruition.

Thank you to my Belonging Co staff and church family for being the most wonderful church to lead. Your prayers and support mean the world. I would like to thank Rachel Koulianos and Paul Bergin for reading through the first stages of the manuscript and pointing me in the right direction. Your insights and feedback were invaluable. A huge thank-you needs to go to my mentor, Pastor Darrell Johnson, who read this book and gave me the most invaluable feedback that helped me immensely.

A huge shout-out goes to my beautiful friends Carla Della Femina, Stephanie Hughes, Destiny Deas, and Nicola Martin, who not only read through the entire manuscript but helped finesse the way the book is articulated. A special thanks goes to my dearest friends who shared their vulnerable and powerful testimonies throughout this book. Without them the book would not be complete.

Thank you to my wonderful executive assistant, Kylie Sullivan, for all your help on this project, and to Avenir, who did a phenomenal job designing the cover. Thank you, of course, to my wonderful acquisition editor, Hanha Parham, for your belief in my voice and this message, and a huge thanks to Lisa Jackson, my brilliant agent, who has believed in me since reading my first-ever proposal.

Notes

Introduction

1. "3875. *paraklétos*," Bible Hub, Strong's Greek Lexical Summary, accessed July 18, 2025, https://biblehub.com/greek/3875.htm.
2. Baker's Evangelical Dictionary of Biblical Theology, s.v. "sanctification," www.biblestudytools.com/dictionaries/bakers-evangelical-disctionary/sanctification.html.

Chapter 1: The Pendulum Swing

1. "7307. *ruach*," Bible Hub, Strong's Hebrew Lexical Summary, accessed July 7, 2025, https://biblehub.com/hebrew/7307.htm.
2. "1577. *ekklésia*," Bible Hub, Strong's Greek Lexical Summary, accessed July 7, 2025, https://biblehub.com/greek/1577.htm.

Chapter 2: Do You Want to Be Well?

1. William Barclay, *The Gospel of John*, vol. 1 The New Daily Study Bible (St. Andrew Press, 1955, 2001), 209.
2. Terry Storch, "John 5:1–15—Paralyzed Mindsets," August 16, 2020, https://terrystorch.com/writing/john-5-paralyzed-mindsets.

Chapter 3: My Best Friend, Holy Spirit

1. Personal conversation with author, 1984.

Chapter 4: Holy Spirit Is Not a What, He's a Who

1. Michael Reeves, *Delighting in the Trinity* (InterVarsity Press, 2012), 90.
2. "Ride on Time," by Black Box, track 6 on *Dreamland*, RCA, 1990.

Chapter 5: The Mother Heart of Father God

1. Anna Golden, "Take It to Jesus," single, 2022.
2. "7307. *ruach*," Bible Hub, Strong's Hebrew Lexical Summary, accessed July 7, 2025, https://biblehub.com/hebrew/7307.htm.
3. Tony Reinke, "Our Mother Who Art in Heaven?," Desiring God, March 4, 2017, https://www.desiringgod.org/articles/our-mother-who-art-in-heaven.
4. John Piper, "God Is Not Male," *Ask Pastor John*, podcast, episode 294, March 10, 2014, https://www.desiringgod.org/interviews/god-is-not-male.
5. "Hokhmah," Encyclopedia.com, accessed July 18, 2025, https://www.encyclopedia.com/environment/encyclopedias-almanacs-transcripts-and-maps/hokhmah.
6. C. S. Lewis, *The Four Loves* (Harcourt, Brace and World, 1960), 31.
7. Sozo Training Guide, Part 1, "Tools for Ministry and for Life," Grace Center, September 20–22, 2012.

Chapter 6: Being Baptized in the Holy Spirit

1. "1411. *dunamis*," Bible Hub, Strong's Greek Lexical Summary, accessed July 18, 2025, https://biblehub.com/greek/1411.htm.
2. Harold W. Hoehner, "Ephesians," in *The Bible Knowledge Commentary: An Exposition of the Scriptures*, vol. 2, eds. J. F. Walvoord and R. B. Zuck (Victor Books, 1985), 620–621.
3. "907. *baptizó*," Bible Hub, Strong's Greek Lexical Summary, accessed November 10, 2025, https://biblehub.com/greek/907.htm.
4. William Barclay, *The Gospel of Matthew*, vol. 2 (Westminster John Knox Press, 2001), 7.
5. *Merriam-Webster Dictionary*, "edify," accessed October 10, 2025, https://www.merriam-webster.com/dictionary/edify.
6. Carl Peterson, "Medical Facts About Speaking in Tongues," *Being Part of the New Covenant*, June 14, 2011, https://

beingunderthenewcovenant.wordpress.com/2011/06/14/medical-facts-about-speaking-in-tongues-—-carl-r-peterson-m-d/.

7. Christopher Dana Lynn et al., "Salivary Alpha-Amylase and Cortisol Among Pentecostals on a Worship and Nonworship Day," *American Journal of Human Biology* 22, no. 6 (2010): 819–22, https://doi.org/10.1002/ajhb.21088.
8. University of Pennsylvania School of Medicine, "Language Center of the Brain Is Not Under Control of Subjects Who 'Speak in Tongues,'" Science Daily, October 31, 2006, www.sciencedaily.com/releases/2006/10/061030183100.htm.

Chapter 7: The Divine Power to Overcome Strongholds

1. *Merriam-Webster Dictionary*, "oppress," accessed July 17, 2025, https://www.merriam-webster.com/dictionary/oppress.
2. Arnold Cole and Pamela Caudill Ovwigho, *Bible Engagement as the Key to Spiritual Growth: A Research Synthesis* (Center for Bible Engagement, 2012), https://d0339759-fa39-4a3b-8db4-c2fa3676bced.filesusr.com/ugd/c59c7d_28c00fc7279a44e8832f15503914c426.pdf.
3. Paul Bergin, *The Path of Presence: A Discipleship of Dwelling with Jesus* (The Belonging Co, 2024), 122.
4. "Knowledge," Bible Hub, accessed July 17, 2025, https://biblehub.com/topical/k/knowlege.htm.

Chapter 8: The Proof Is in the Pudding

1. Kenneth Branagh, dir., *Cinderella*, Disney movie, 2015.

Chapter 9: Learning to Know His Voice

1. "1827. *demamah*," Bible Hub, Strong's Hebrew Lexical Summary, accessed July 18, 2025, https://biblehub.com/hebrew/1827.htm.
2. Te Rautini, "Peace/Afio Mai," *Kia Kaha*, copyright 2017.

Chapter 10: Living a Spirit-Led Life

1. Darrell W. Johnson, *Fifty-Seven Words That Change the World: A Journey Through the Lord's Prayer* (2021), 98.
2. *Merriam-Webster Dictionary*, "hematidrosis," accessed July 18, 2025, https://www.merriam-webster.com/medical/hematidrosis.

About the Author

Alex Seeley was born and raised in Australia and spent seventeen years pastoring there. It is also where she met and married her husband, Henry. After relocating to Nashville in 2012, they founded The Belonging Co, a church where they minister together to thousands of people each week. She is a passionate teacher of the Word with the unique ability to reveal how the Word of God is applicable to our everyday lives.